WARNING!

WARNING!

REALITY MAY NOT BE
COMPATIBLE WITH
YOUR WORLDVIEW

P. A. RANSOM

ARCHWAY
PUBLISHING

Archway Publishing books may be ordered through booksellers or by contacting:

Archway Publishing
1663 Liberty Drive
Bloomington, IN 47403
www.archwaypublishing.com
1 (888) 242-5904

ISBN: 978-1-4808-7301-8 (sc)
ISBN: 978-1-4808-7300-1 (e)

Library of Congress Control Number: 2018914906

Print information available on the last page.

Archway Publishing rev. date: 01/03/2019

INTRODUCTION

The most significant event in all mankind's history was the awakening of intellectual consciousness, and the ability to make informed decisions based on careful observation, logic, and critical reasoning.

We all live in a world that is constructed in the mind. Our senses tell us that the world is real. We just accept as fact that what our senses reveal to us is not an illusion. Have you have ever been to a magic show and seen a master illusionist defy the laws of physics, and everything you believed to be true about reality? Trompe l'oeil (trump loi) "fool the eye" paintings are masterful murals that appear on walls, floors, and ceilings, to create what seems to be real. In radio days, artificial sounds were produced to augment programing. If you have seen or heard any of these illusions, you know how easily the brain can be deceived. What we think we know is sometimes far from the truth.

All stimuli we receive is filtered through the brain, and it is the brain that tells us what is real and what is not. Our minds are a vast repository of all the knowledge, sensations, and assumptions we have accumulated over the span of a lifetime. We are forever chasing reality; however, it seems to be a never ending and elusive quarry.

Many thoughts that inundate the mind seem to have no pattern or purpose. They contain daydreams, fantasies, extrapolations, and many forms of mental garbage. These are the voices inside our head. When we try to turn these voices off they seem to keep up an incessant dialog. Have you ever had a song in your mind that keeps repeating over and over in an endless loop? These voices are forever describing and reinforcing our assumptions about reality.

Our perception of existence and reality is no more than the interactions of nerve tissues in the brain and the chemistry which interfaces with them. Their activation unites these neural circuits, and they eventually support our thoughts and feelings. All internal and external stimuli are self-grounded and begin and end in the brain. These stimuli shape and influence the dynamics of our daily lives. They reflect our passions and prejudices, our regard for the environment and the world. The way in which we interpret these stimuli is the very essence of who we are.

When we search for the eternal questions of the ages we sometimes reach out for abstract or spiritual ideals. Our mind seems to take on a spiritual awareness as we probe the concepts of God, truth, and justice. These things cannot be experienced directly through the senses; they are abstract concepts that do not exist in the physical world but are psychogenetic in nature.

If we are to have any understanding of the issues we all face, we must remember that no matter how well thought out our knowledge it is always subject to change as our understanding evolves.

We must be wary, for the world is full of people who would attempt to usurp our thoughts with their values and beliefs. When we examine our own thoughts, we begin to question the voices of others. When we do this, our mind is no longer cluttered by their thoughts and assumptions. It is important what we believe, but it is more important to know why we believe the way we do.

In this synthesis I present to you, the reader, some of the ways I think we might separate reality from superstition and irrational thought. It is your responsibility to edit the content of these ideas. Some of you may have divergent views and some may not. There is always an antithesis to every idea. My purpose is to get you to think critically, use reason, and a little common sense. I am sure that there is something herein that will offend some readers. This is only natural because we all have different life experiences and world views. It is up to you to determine what has merit and what does not.

CONTENTS

PART 3

PART 1

PREHISTORIC AND ANCIENT MAN

The history of primitive man in a hunter gatherer society is a story of survival. He was set upon by wild beasts and pummeled by the elements, over which he had no control or comprehension. It was a world that did not favor the life of our primitive ancestors. Primitive man was not aware of the unseen microscopic world nor the vastness of the cosmos. As early man went about his daily life, survival was the most important consideration.

Prehistoric man thought that natural objects and events were caused by unseen spirits or gods and that they inhabited the mountains, rivers, and skies. They were thought to be responsible for controlling natural phenomena. Primitive man in search of an explanation looked to the supernatural. He gave names and accounts to the mysteries that were beyond his control. These spirits morphed into the primitive religion of Animism, which gave a spirit to plants, animals, and natural occurrences.

These spirits had to be appeased lest bad luck befall the offender. The shaman was regarded as one who could exert influence on the emanation of spiritual forces and act as a medium between those spirits and the real world. He used magic rituals and incantations to heal the sick and ward off evil spirits. The shaman was able, while in a trance or altered state, to leave the body and travel to the spirit world, where he could communicate with beings that resided on a supernatural plain of existence. The shaman sought a spiritual ally to restore balance to emotional and physical distress. These spirits had to be appeased by offerings, incantations, and ritual practices.

Primitive man had little in the way of technology: no telescopes, microscopes, or computers. Despite these disadvantages, man had some remarkable achievements. We can look through a telescope today and see the vastness of our universe. We can look down a microscope and see the enormous complexity of the unseen world. The computer gives us a great advantage in the calculating, retrieving, and storage of information.

A water microscope invented in China about 4,000 years ago was capable of magnification of about 150 times. The movement of stars and planets was charted with a high degree of accuracy. The Incan practice of trepanation, a type of brain surgery, was performed with a high measure of success. Many of these surgeries were performed more than 1,000 years ago. The concept of zero was invented by the Babylonians and the Incas, independently of the other. The pre-Columbian civilizations of Mesoamerica were Stone Age cultures, and without metal tools or draft animals, they produced magnificent architecture. Ancient people were just as intelligent as we moderns; however, they were not blessed with the wealth of knowledge, the benefits of scientific revelation, and the technical marvels we have today.

THE BRAIN

The brain is a product of evolution. It developed over millions of years and was designed by evolutionary forces to sense and respond to the environment. The modern human brain developed about 200,000 years ago as we began to live in groups, develop culture, make tools, and form social relationships. Evolution is still changing the brain to cope with its environment. Who knows what alterations might be in our future?

Peter Russell explains in *The Brain Book* that the brain contains approximately 10 billion neurons, which is about as many stars as in the Milky Way galaxy. Each neuron can have as many as ten thousand connections, so the total number of synapses could be as high as 100 trillion.

Synapses are chemical switches that route electrical impulses from one nerve cell to another. All this is contained in a lump of matter that weighs about three pounds. The brain outperforms even the most advanced computers in its power and speed. It is little wonder it is regarded as the most complicated lump of matter in the known universe.

Regardless of what our senses reveal to us, it is the interaction of neurons in our brains that creates what we think is reality. Our brain receives millions of bits of information every minute. We organize these signals in accordance with their importance, and it reveals to us our reality.

The brain is truly a multitasking device. It regulates the nervous system, circulatory system, reproduction, respiratory, digestive tracts, and muscles. These bodily systems work together to ensure a vital functioning unit with the brain as the central controlling device. Our thoughts set off a succession of cellular reactions that influence the mind and body, and together they create an interplay with the outside world. The brain keeps the entire body and mental processes in a state of balance. The brain is also a part of reality. The mind is the result of electrical impulses as they move around the brain, giving rise to emotions, memories, and experiences. The mind is without a measurable dimension, and it has no locus known to science. Many people think that the mind and brain are synonymous.

Every man-made thing begins as a concept in the brain, and we can shape things in the world of objects. Mathematician and science historian Jacob Boronski (1908–1974) wrote in his book *The Ascent of Man* that "the hand is the cutting edge of the mind."

What the mind can visualize, the hand can produce—but only within the universal physical laws of nature. Visualization is a technique for creating mental images that help give clarity to our thoughts. We can create through manual manipulation what we can visualize, but only as the laws of physical nature dictate. Objects in the subjective world have no substance and can only be manipulated in the mind. We can build a house, but we cannot build an angel. Angels are noncorporeal and without substance, they can only be manipulated in the mind. The same could be said of gods, devils, pixies, and gnomes.

Have you ever tried to dispatch pesky little flies that keep annoying you? If so, you know how quick and elusive they can be. With brains calculated to be about five hair breadths long and two across, their reflexes are lightning fast. Their small brains control the same bodily functions as ours. They have, for millions of years, gone about the business of flydom unabated with no need of a larger brain. They are reactionary biological units and act only in accordance with their genetic makeup. One can only imagine the power of a brain the size of ours!

The brain can do many amazing things. It can entertain abstract thoughts, express those thoughts in language, remember, and pass on that information to others. It can do a myriad of other things while carrying out a balance between the mental and physical states of being. All this is done while coordinating all the things necessary in our daily lives. The brain is aware of the positioning of all body parts as they interact with the outside world. This awareness is known as body schema. We know the position of our limbs and are aware of the extension of all our senses. These schemas act as a basic conceptual structure that allows us to move effortlessly in our environment. The brain constructs a likeness of reality complete with the shape, color, and its location in time and space.

Every thought and emotion creates a pathway in your neural network. Each time these thoughts and emotions are repeated, they become hardwired in the brain, which makes them easier to recall. This repetition is learning through rote, and it establishes quick and easy path ways to memory. However, learning by rote does not guarantee understanding.

As wonderful as the brain is, it has several basic flaws. There is nothing in the brain that tells us something is correct or distinguishes right from wrong or real from delusional. There is no self-correcting mechanism that can recognize or identify truth. Our brains are pattern-seeking devices. The brain does not give an absolute and accurate picture of reality, but a model representation. It looks only for patterns of recognition and often constructs patterns that are not there. Our visual focus is no larger than a postage stamp held at arm's length. As we move our gaze about, our brains seamlessly construct what we perceive as reality.

The brain depends on the senses to reveal to us what is real and what is not. We often entertain flawed memories and beliefs;

they lie to us and lead us to false conclusions that have little to do with reality.

Cognitive biases are a deviation from rationality and, can lead to defective thinking. They include prejudices, social biases, stereotyping, memory errors, and heuristics, all of which might lead to an unintentional divergence from the truth. There are many other belief biases that can affect a logical evaluation and conclusion. The old reptilian brain, or brain stem, is the oldest part of the brain. It can interfere with logical and rational thought.

Fallacies distort our assumptions and present to us false images about the world. We rely on our memories, believing them to be accurate, but they are only our minds' flawed reconstructions of past events. Our minds are overflowing with prejudices and biases of every description. It is only through careful analysis and scrutiny that we can hope to arrive at some semblance of truth.

We must remember that no matter how well thought out our knowledge, it is always subject to change as our understanding evolves. If we become lazy and do not logically analyze our belief systems, we may be basing our lives on faulty assumptions that are devoid of any reality. If we do not practice self-analysis, we might find ourselves in a morass of delusional thought that keeps building on one false assumption after another until one's whole life is filled with illogical beliefs.

The functioning of the brain is the very essence of our existence. It is responsible for all we think and do. When the brain dies, it is the end of our individuality, our personages, and our personalities. There is no credible evidence that after death there is any after life.

CONSCIOUSNESS

Consciousness is that state which gives rise to all we think and feel, and is an awareness in both body and mind. It gives us the perception of ourselves and the world around us. We are aware of things that affect the body, such as pain, pleasure, hunger, anger, and a multitude of other sensations. There is a world of the mind that encompasses our inner thoughts, fantasies, and remembrances. There are also events of perceiving the reality of the external world, things that excite the senses, sights, sounds, and things that are related to touch. Consciousness is an awareness of the physical world, the location, movement, speed, shape, size, and direction of objects. Consciousness is a tag-along function of the mind and is only a perception of the things that relate to the self. We can only experience our own consciousness and not those of others.

Consciousness is an unfolding process. When we are born there is little conscious awareness. When we begin to explore our world as toddlers, a whole new range of experiences opens to us. At this age we are directly involved in the observation, perception, and participation of the new-found world before us. This is an exciting and wonderful time. It seems a never-ending chore for parents as they try to keep the child safe from harm. As we mature more objects and experiences are revealed to us. Age tells us that the evolution of our consciousness is an ongoing process. Learning seems effortless. Our brains build pathways of language, abstract thought, and even spirituality. All these things seem to unite and meld into this one thing we call consciousness.

We are not merely mechanisms which react to stimuli; we have developed the ability to control our own experiences. We can plan for and project our minds into the future. Without this ability we could only obey the instructions and programs given to us by our genes. We can make our own decisions without genetic interference or instructions.

Animals also have a high degree of consciousness about things in and around their environment. Animals don't seem to have spiritually or abstract thought, but only that which their genes give them to survive and reproduce. Even the lowest of life forms seem to react in some way to their environment, but this reaction is only gene related. At this level there seems to be no self-awareness as we know it.

There is no one place in the brain where consciousness can be found. There have been many books and articles written about consciousness. However, it seems to be a subject that deftly avoids defining its essential nature.

WORDS AND LANGUAGE

There are more than 6000 languages spoken worldwide. The concepts and basis on that which we define our world is language. Words which comprise language are concepts that represent persons, places, things, ideas, and actions. When put together, words describe a representation of our thoughts, and through vocalization allow us to communicate with one another. The language we speak shapes the way we see the world. People who speak different languages do think differently. Language is a uniquely human gift. Animals might sound an alarm, or growl their displeasure at something, but using language as an instrument of abstract thought is beyond their mental aptitude. However, some Chimpanzees when properly trained have mastered an impressive vocabulary through signing and arranging blocks with words to form simple sentences.

Words and language serve to describe the placement of things in time and space. The word, no matter the language, brings fourth the image of what it represents. The word house in English, and casa in Spanish, as well as other languages, bring fourth the image and concept of a dwelling place. The word fire brings fourth the image of the yellow, red and blue flames dancing, smoke, and glowing coals, but it has no warmth or light to give us. If we want to know fire, we must engage it directly through the senses. Empirical knowledge is gained only by experience and is not derived by rational or logical thought.

Words only represent and classify the world and our actions within it. Objective reality exists outside the realm of vocalization. Words have no meaning outside our state of consciousness. Words and language are only used to symbolize and communicate ideas. Sign language, used by the hearing impaired, is a rich and impressive way to communicate. It consists of a variety of movements, finger spelling, hand and body gestures, and facial expressions. Many of these expressions convey ideas and concepts, rather than words. Most of us use hand and body movements to augment speech. We might hold our nose to indicate an unpleasant smell, give a hand shake upon meeting, or wave good-by as a parting gesture. There is a myriad of other signals used by people to augment their vocalization.

Language can be used to deceive as well as instruct. "Doublespeak", is language that says the opposite of what is true. This language deliberately distorts the meanings of words to give respectability to words that are inherently distasteful. The words in doublespeak are not to convey meaning, but to distort it. This kind of language is sometimes referred to as "Orwellian language", it hides the lie and its true intention is to misrepresent the facts by words that mean the opposite.

(George Orwell, English author, published in1949 a novel entitled 1984)

Orwell's novel pictured a bleak and dystopian place called Oceania, ruled by an authoritarian state that practiced surveillance, deception, and the alteration of history. The thought police, through listening devices and hidden cameras, pursue independent thought that does not conform to the ideas of the state. There are portraits everywhere warning that the party leader, "Big Brother", is watching you. Sometimes I wonder if big brother is watching us. The use of surveillance cameras is ubiquitous, and they can be found most everywhere. It seems we are always being watched and our image recorded. Employers use them to monitor workers use of time, and to check for pilfering. Law enforcement uses these devices to track the movements of suspected criminals, and anything else they might find unlawful.

There are word traps that have the look of truth, but closer examination renders them false. Politicians are notorious for their furtive use of language. Example: We will make medical care available to all our citizens. The truth is that medical care is already available to all our citizens. Availability does not mean affordability. You may not be able to afford it or have the resources to purchase the protection of insurance. The clean air act is anything but clean allowing the biggest polluters to carry on business as usual. Words like clean air are specious and Orwellian. They hide the lie, and their true intent is misrepresented by words that mean the opposite. Don't discredit yourself by using Orwellian language. The Patriot Act is another good example of Orwellian language. This legislation takes away many of our civil rights, and who would dare to be against patriotism? We must always be on guard against coded and encrypted statements which have special meanings directed to specific groups. Pretentious and bombastic language may be used to purposefully confuse those people whose lack of education, or upbringing does not render meaning to the words that are used. Lying with the use of polls and statistics or making a point by the association of familiar idioms are other traps of which we should be aware. Paradoxical language is also confusing. "Look before you leap" seems to be good advice, as does "he who hesitates is lost". Lying by omission of pertinent facts can further confuse the listener. This could lead to false conclusions. Always be on guard. Everyone who speaks has his or her own way of expressing ideas. The listener hears and understands only that which falls within their frame of reference, or range of experiences. What one hears and believes is often judged by others to be hypocrisy. Example:

Our vision is to bring freedom and democracy to the Middle East. As a divergent view many people in that region of the world view this as Imperialism and occupation. Does truth lie somewhere between the two extremes? There may be other viable considerations. Always seek a third explanation when you are presented with only two alternatives.

Beware of people who claim the right to control the definitions of words and phrases. Their goal is to gain power over your mind. If everyone in the world believed the same thing we would still have to question its validity. If we are to truly to understand what someone is saying, we must also understand his or her motives and hidden agendas. These motives may be benign, unsound, or offensive to reason. Choose your words carefully.

WORLDVIEW

A worldview is the way in which one perceives the world. It is a mental and basic understanding of how the universe works, and it takes many forms. It is a set of assumptions about reality. A world view is a combination of philosophies, scientific facts, theories, and religious opinions. They are composed of axioms, stories, memes, and cultural ideas. These beliefs all unite into a whole that the individual bases their actions and lives upon. Often these beliefs are based on sacred books, scrolls, religious dogma, and teachings of individuals who profess to know the true nature of reality. They are also based on scientific truths, and the scientific method of discovery. All these many beliefs in various proportions are a blueprint of one's worldview.

A world view should encompass a valid way to see reality, without fleeing into a world of superstition, ignorance, and irrational thought. We must apply knowledge of the world we know by careful observation, logic, and critical reasoning, as well as creative and intuitive thought. When our species first became aware and questioned the world; our senses revealed a perplexing view of the world and all things that make up our existence. There were many things that seemed out of control and begging for an explanation. Without the understanding of a more advanced explanation, primitive man moved toward the supernatural; and bestowed upon all things a spiritual nature, that they might understand and explain the mysteries of their world. To them the animals, plants, all geological formations, and forces had a spirit. These beliefs became the religion of Animism. Prayer and sacrifices were given to appease the spirits for any transgressions that might offend them. This is probably the first worldview of our primitive ancestors.

These primitive beliefs morphed into the many Gods of polytheistic cultures. The existence of these Gods explained many mysteries and gave birth to the new religious paradigm of many gods. The gods of ancient Greece, Rome, and Egypt are probably the best known. Many of these ancient religions have taken hold in modern times and constitute a Worldview which encompasses a belief of many Gods. The best place to start understanding world views is to begin by analyzing your own. Are you harboring any beliefs that are inconsistent with reality?

Deism is the world view that God created the universe, and that it was left to function on its own. The deist does not think that prayer has the power to produce any effect on the physical world. There are no religious dogmas, rituals, or sacred texts. The universe operates on the universal laws of physics, with no interference of outside forces. God can only be known by the study of science and nature.

Theism is the world view that God created the universe, and all things in it. God watches over his creation and is free to interfere with its operation. He judges his creations and rewards or punishes those who please or displease him. God is omnipresent, omnipotent, and has knowledge of all things past, present, and future. This world view is prevalent among revealed religions. The good life is to glorify God, submit to his will, and live one's life according to the scriptures.

An agnostic world view is one in which nothing can be known of the existence or the nature of God. An agnostic does not believe in divinely inspired texts, revealed word, or miracles that are contrary to natural law. The agnostic reserves judgment on things that are not proven.

Belief in only one God was a new concept to the Egyptian people. The Pharaoh Akhenaten proclaimed a one God religion with the sun representing that God. Upon his death, all traces of this one Sun God were stricken from statues, representations, and inscriptions. The Egyptian people returned to the worship of many gods. This was probably one of the first one God worldviews.

The appearance of Abrahamic monotheism expresses a covenant with God to believe in and worship only him. This includes his power, justice, and mercy over all his creation.

Islam is the total submission to Allah, the one true God. He is all powerful, all knowing, and the creator, sustainer, and judge of his creation.

God is the creator of Universe and all things in it. The Christian views the world from a biblical standpoint. Salvation is obtained through Jesus Christ, who was sent by God, and died for our sins. The bible is a guide to living a good Christian life.

Judaism and Islam do not consider Christianity as a Monotheistic religion, the worship of God the father and Jesus the son exclude it as a monotheistic Worldview.

Pantheism is the view that the universe and all it contains is divine. It is a deterministic Worldview that follows cause and effect as the prime mover. There are no personal Gods, and no life after death. Death is the end of your existence; you only meld into the elements from whence you came.

Naturalism is the belief that only natural laws and forces operate in the universe without intervention of the supernatural.

Nihilism is a rejection of all religions and that life has no meaning. Nothing has any value. There is only matter and the forces that act upon it in a closed system.

Existentialism is a philosophy that transcends Nihilism. People are free and responsible for their actions in an indifferent universe.

New Age thought is a combination of religious and spiritual beliefs which are drawn from a variety of sources. The followers are generally people who are dedicated to the pursuit of mystical interpretations of reality. The New Age movement usually rejects traditional religions and looks to practices regarded as pseudo-science. Most New Age thought is an inaccurate understanding of how reality works.

There are many other world views besides those mentioned here, Hinduism, Buddhism, Shinto, Jainism, and Confucianism, to name just a very few.

A worldview is a set of ideas that are held in the mind and evolve as we discover new ideas to augment or replace old ones. Many of the views and assumptions that are supported in the mind have no credence and are carried only by emotional appeal. Some people go with what they want to be true, not what they know to be true. Always be careful that you are not entertaining flawed or unrealistic logic in your worldview. Reason requires that we do not fall into superstitious or fallacious ideas. Natural laws are always independent of any human will.

THE GOD PROBLEM

Everyone who believes in God has a concept in their mind of his inherent characteristics. These concepts have usually been passed down to us by our parents, our guardians, and our culture. Social indoctrination into the faith starts at a very young age, and it continues to be reinforced as we mature. We continue to absorb in our minds, stories, rituals, and dogmas related to our religion. We have little choice but to accept these broadly circulated narratives of our religious faith. When people begin to question the absurdity of these stories it frees our minds of the superstitions that block rational thought. We must take a giant step and realize that the mind is the controlling device that leads us into rational and orderly relationships. It is the mind that holds the concept of God. Each person has their own thoughts as to the nature of God. No matter what image of a transcendent entity is formulated it is held in the brain and is no more than a series of electrical impulses between neurons.

God is a concept and a creation of the human mind. Why should we seek outside the mind to find him? When we pray, is to our own imagination, and do we worship our own psyche?

Does God answer prayer? To the true believer God does answer prayer; however, prayers have been offered by every religion in every age to live in peace. These many trillions of prayers have fallen on deaf ears. Perhaps God does not find us worthy to live in peace. Conceivably the silence is saying no to these many prayers. The atheist might say there is no one to hear your prayers and that God is just a figment of the human imagination. Atheists seem intent on disproving the existence of God, the bible, and anything of a religious nature.

Madalyn Murray O'Hare (The American Atheist) "Atheism may be defined as the mental attitude which unreservedly accepts the supremacy of reason and aims at establishing a lifestyle and ethical outlook verifiable by experience and the scientific method independent of arbitrary assumptions of authority and creeds."

The infallibility of God is a question that seems to test the utmost limits of credibility. It seems that no matter what happens God is left off the hook. When a sick child is cured, God has shown his mercy. If the child dies, God needs that child in heaven. Who are we to question Gods will? We will all be united in heaven and know the mind of God.

People can believe what they want but must not spread superstitious and erroneous ideas. Our public schools and government must be kept free of religious and destructive concepts least we fall into the shoals of dystopian thought.

A PAGAN CHRIST?

The Rosetta stone was found in AD1799 during the Napoleonic wars, by a French Captain named Pierre Bouchard. The stone was written in two languages, Greek and Egyptian, and it was scribed in three different writing styles Greek, hieroglyphic, and demotic. Demotic was a script used by the ordinary Egyptian people.

Thomas Young and Jean-Francois Champollion worked independently to decipher the Egyptian hieroglyphic characters inscribed on the stone. In 1814 Young identified the name of the king Ptolemy, and Champollion followed in1822 breaking the hieroglyphic code. This discovery ended over 2000 years of darkness in which little was known about Egyptian culture or religion. The god Horus predates the arrival of Jesus by some 2000 years. There are scores of inherent characteristics that are similar in both the Horus and Jesus mythology. The bible, it is said, copied the myth of Horus and gives to Jesus the same attributes. The virgin birth, the miracles, and resurrection, are all taken from the pagan myths of Horus, Attis, Dionysus, Mithra, Krishna, and Buddha, as well as others. These attributes seem to mimic one another and are all antecedent to the Jesus myth.

A firestorm erupted between Christianity and the newly discovered Egyptian culture. Champollion deftly told the clergy that the great flood occurred before the Egyptian civilization, and there was no conflict with the biblical account. Religious Christians take the gospels in the bible as reliable historical events and literal truth. The life of Jesus comes to us through the Gospels of the bible. There seems to be no historical records of Jesus outside the gospels.

There is much information on the web, both pro and con, about the origin of the Jesus myth. Each appears to have some acceptance. It is up to you to decide which has credence, and which does not. The final assessment is yours.

GALILEO GALILEI, ISAAC NEWTON, ALBERT EINSTEIN, & NIKOLA TESLA

Melchior, Casper, and Balthasar the three kings, or magi of biblical lore, gave the Christ child, gold, frankincense, and myrrh. These kings discovered the Messiah and worshiped him as their savior. This Christmas story has been retold many times, and the discovery of the messiah was their gift to the world.

Galileo, Newton, and Einstein are the three wise men who brought us from the ignorance of the dark ages, and into the light and understanding of our reality.

Galileo Galilei (1564-1642) was an astronomer, mathematician, philosopher, and physicist. In1609 he learned of an optical invention that made distant objects seem closer. He soon improved on the invention to the point of 30 times magnification. When he began to train his invention on the heavens, a whole new sphere of unknown heavenly bodies was revealed to him. His subsequent publication, in the Sidereal Messenger, a little book that soon made him famous. Copernican theory that the sun was at the center of the of the solar system was against church doctrine. Galileo argued for the Copernican theory although it was against the teachings of the Holy Catholic church. Galileo was eventually convicted of heresy and was placed under house arrest for the rest of his life. Galileo

will be remembered for piercing the vail of ignorance, and opening
the heavens to scientific study and discovery.

Isaac Newton (1643-1727) at age 12 he was enrolled at the king's
school in Grantham where he studied chemistry. Newton was enrolled in the University of Cambridge's Trinity College, which at
that time was infused in Aristotelian philosophy. Newton, however, was interested in the more modern philosophers.

Cambridge closed in 1665 due to the plague. Newton returned
home and studied on his own for 18 months. During this time, he
formulated his ideas on calculus, and how light acted when passed
through a prism, produced the colors of the rainbow. The falling
apple sparked his notions about the laws of gravity. Newton formulated the conceptual structure of what many considered the greatest of all scientific accomplishments the (Mathematical Principles
of Natural Philosophy) more commonly known as the Principia.
It lay unpublished until 1687. Newton was reluctant to publish his
works and kept his findings mostly to himself.

Newton was very religious and thought he could discover the
nature of God through his scientific work. He worked more on
the bible and religion than on science and became obsessed with
alchemy. Newton's aim was to find the philosopher's stone which
would reveal to him the true nature of God.

Newton is best known for the publication of the Principia,
which explained the movement of heavenly bodies, and the three
physical laws which were the foundation of classical mechanics.
Newton's discovery that light was composed of constituent colors
when passed through a prism and was reconstituted back into white
light when passed through a second prism. He invented the reflect-
ing telescope and developed calculus at age 23. He was knighted by
Queen Anne in1705.

Albert Einstein (1879-1955, scientist, and physicist) developed
the general theory of relativity. He won the Nobel Prize for physics
in 1921. In 1905 Einstein came up with the equation E=mc2, the

equation that propelled him into world prominence. It stated that minuscule particles of matter could be converted into a massive amount of energy; and thus, the atomic age came to prominence.

Einstein was a pacifist, and after the bombing of Hiroshima in Japan, he became a major player against the use of the atomic bomb. He maintained that it should be used only as a determent against war. He continued to work on a unified field theory, and general relativity until his death in 1955.

Nikola Tesla (1856-1943), If he is right, has turned upside down everything we ever thought we knew about reality. Tesla was one of the most innovative men who ever lived. He is responsible for most of the electronic devices we use today, and they can be traced to Tesla's inventions. Alternating current, lasers, remote control, and limitless free energy, all sprang from his mind.

Tesla thought in terms of energy, frequency, and vibrations. He thought that the theory of gravity was false, and it is electro magnetism, and magnetic lines of force that allows the planets to orbit each other. Tesla believed that there were magnetic lines of force that lay in what is thought to be empty space.

After Tesla's death in 1943 the FBI classified and confiscated all his papers. The papers disappeared, and no one knows where they are today. One can only imagine what information they might reveal. Free energy for everyone in the world? If energy were free to everyone, who would have the most to lose?

WHAT IS REALITY?

We cannot know reality without exploring memory. Without memory there would be no way to formulate a point of reference. It is memory that gives substance to the self, and it is memory which gives our lives meaning and continuity. Memory is something we start developing at birth, or perhaps even in the womb. We learn as our brains establish new pathways between old memories and new experiences. We can walk from one room to another because we know by the senses, and by memory the reality of its limited range in time and space. Memories are the thoughts we carry in our minds and are one of the tools we use in the thinking process. The language and words we have learned help us to form a mental picture of our memories.

Our brain produces mental pictures while dreaming. Lucid dreams seem quite real, but they are only our brains making up stories. These stories are the brains way of bringing a kind of continuity to the random firing of neutrons as we sleep. We rarely remember these dreams as we go about our daily lives. Sometimes new insights are gained, and we awaken only to find that during sleep a dream has solved a problem for us.

Our memories flow to us through our neural network and reveal to us what seems to be reality. Without the links of memory all thought would have to start at a zero point. The association of memories helps us to recognize remembered experiences and organize our thoughts.

Reality exists in two fundamental modes; it is an underlying way we perceive the impressions of what we think is reality. These modes, or forms are introduced to us as objective and subjective reality.

When we developed conscious thought and became self-aware, we separated ourselves from the natural world. It is this perception that has spawned dualism. We are not separate, but just a part of everything that exists. Dualism is only an illusion. Objective physical reality does not emanate from the mind nor does it in any way depend upon what we think.

The subjective world is one of thought and is a manifestation of the brain. It is the world of logic, math, language, unicorns, leprechauns, ghosts, goblins, angels, devils, and flights of fancy. There are incredible worlds of beauty, light, and love, and every adventure you can imagine. These things are all produced in the brain, and only exist in the mind. They have no substance in the physical world and are psychogenetic in nature.

We can never be sure what reality is, because our senses do not cover the full range of possible experiences. There is a break which lies between our human senses, unseen, unfelt, and vacuous of our experiences. With only our five senses we try to make sense of our complex universe. The five senses do not cover the full spectrum or the range of possible experiences; they only cover the range within the threshold of human detection. Our senses limit our perception, and we experience only the surface of reality. There is a range of light frequencies outside our visual perception, and vibrations beyond our auditory range. Many of earth's species are aware of elements in their environment that are unknown to us. Each creature experiences the reality of their world from their own extension. The old proverbial saying about not being able to see the forest for the trees illustrates this conundrum of our perception. We see only objects and not the whole. The force of gravity is unseen and unheard, but it influences everything we do. We live in an ocean of air that pushes in on us from all sides, but we take little notice except on a windy day.

The world is constantly changing. To reexamine our beliefs from time to time would seem to be the prudent thing to do. When we embrace ignorance and turn our backs on reality, we close our minds to new ideas and discoveries.

Isaac Newton was not the first to use the metaphor, "If I have seen further it is by standing on the shoulders of giants."

There is no mistaking his meaning. Those that have gone before us are the trailblazers who make possible all the knowledge we have today. If we had to discover everything on our own, where do you think we would we be today?

Newtonian physics, sometimes called classical mechanics, is a deterministic science that governs the movement of physical bodies in an objective world. The movement and position of these bodies can be determined at any point in time and space. This is the world we know by careful observation, analysis, and experimentation.

At the subatomic level, there are no solid objects. It is at this point that Newtonian physics break down. The old clockwork universe does not work at the subatomic level, and we find ourselves in an aberrant and unfamiliar universe of chance and possibilities. Waves and particles have no attributes of their own, they only share the identity of the systems with which they interact. Everything in the universe is a complex series of interconnected relationships that create matter as we know it. The cosmos is a seething cauldron of energy and matter. It is all interconnected in ever changing structure, and relationships. When these subatomic particles come together they form matter, and act according to Newtonian laws of physics.

Science has invented instruments that have pushed our limitations far beyond our natural powers of perception. The microscope lets us see the world of the very small. The telescope gives us a glimpse of our universe and beyond. Yet we are bound by our physical restraints to be tethered to this world. This world is a part of the absolute total of everything; of which we are only a small part.

In 1814 (Pierre Simon Laplace, French philosopher and mathematician) published an article on scientific determinism. It states that if an intelligence knew all the forces that set nature in motion and knew all the positions of nature in the world, and the movement of bodies in the universe, it could be stated in a single formula that would reveal to us the past, present, and future.

Our consciousness and our senses continually present the world to us as separate unrelated objects. Our focus and perception are centered in the self and the ego, which only allows us to experience the world from a self-grounded reality. It is this narrow way of seeing that gives us the illusion that we are separate from every other thing. Data from our five senses are sent to the brain where it is decoded in accordance with our previous experiences and memories. The brain tries to make sense of these sensory inputs, and it reveals to us reality as we know it.

When we use the scientific method to examine a specimen, the specimen, the environment, and the examiner all influence each other. When a specimen is removed from its environment it no longer acts in its usual way. A fish out of water does not swim; water is an essential part of the equation. Water takes on the shape of its container, which is the nature of water. Gravity acts upon the water to hold it in place, otherwise it would have no restraints. The examiner brings to the equation his or her own expectations and prejudices. The examiner's environment also constrains and restricts in much the same way.

If you are searching for immortality look no further, it has been with you all along. Death is only a metamorphosis, a melding with the eternal cosmos. It is a part of you that merely changes from one form to another

Marcus Aurelias, (Roman Emperor from 161 to 180) wrote in

his book Meditations "That which has died does not drop out of the universe. If it stays here, it also changes here, and is dissolved in to its proper parts, which are elements of the universe and of yourself, and these too change, and murmur not."

Do we manufacture reality in our minds? Are we always searching for reality? Do we ever see the hidden whole, or the plexus of interconnectedness? Do we exist only in the mind? There seems to be more questions than answers.

FREE WILL

What is free will? Freewill is a freedom of choice that is not determined by prior causes, or divine intervention. No discussion of free will can take place without an understanding of predestination. Predestination is the doctrine of events that are preordained, and over which we have no control. God's governance over his creation in all its aspects is divine intervention. Christianity, Islam, and Judaism all view God as a supreme being. God, it is believed, is omnipotent, omnipresent, and omniscient. If God is omniscient he knows in unison everything that is past, present, and in the future. Foreknowledge of everything, and his power to intervene at any time or place would negate free will. If God knows how we will choose, how can we choose otherwise? If we are free to choose and God does not know our choices he is not omniscient. If God cannot intervene in our lives, he is not omnipotent. This seems to be a direct contradiction of the concept of God. Some might argue that God exists outside time and space, and there is no contradiction between his divine providence and omniscience. This is sometimes called divine infallibility. Time has no meaning in a balanced system of equilibrium. If God is omniscient he must know this system to set it in motion. This is known to us as the laws of cause and effect. Any causal system known by God would negate free will because it would be predestined. If God interfered into the laws of cause and effect, these newly created events would also negate free will.

Our knowledge is limited to our memories and is formed by matching with known patterns and events. If our free will is limited by the laws of nature and physical reality we would not be able to will anything unless we could set it in motion. To set something in motion requires a mental consideration, and a physical action. To influence anything by will alone is just an illusion.

Fatalism is a philosophy that negates free will. It assumes that we have no control over the events in our lives, and that everything is preordained. Karma posits that each deed, good or bad, is returned to us in kind in this lifetime or the next. We are reincarnated that we might learn from our mistakes in a future life or be destined to repeat future lives in an endless cycle of death and rebirth.

Every event has a cause and sets in motion a chain of events over which we have no control. If this is true, the laws of cause and effect would seem to be absolute. How can we be held ethically and morally responsible for anything over which we have no control? Free will and Determinism have been at odds with each other for centuries. Each one seems to be plausible, or is this just another perplexing enigma?

MEMES

In his book, (The Selfish Gene (1976) British evolutionary biologist Richard Dawkins) coined the word "meme" to describe viruses of the mind that replicate and spread ideas.

Memes include speech, writing, and a multitude of things that can be passed from one mind to another. That song that keeps repeating over and over in your mind, the prayers you learned in church, that catch phrase advertising some product, and a myriad of other things that inundate the mind are all memes.

A meme is information or an action which is copied and passed on from one mind to another, then replicated and passed on again and again like an infectious virus. Some are toxic ideas and others are benign. A meme does not differentiate between what is good or bad, or what is useful or not, its only reason to exist is to replicate and pass on its information.

The meme is a human replicator; humans are unique because our brains are wired to imitate and copy. One meme can build upon another and in this way, it becomes an evolutionary algorithm, spreading and copying information as it moves from one brain to another. Religion is a good example. As theological ideas form and shift they provide us with different systems of belief, dogmas, and rituals. This accounts for the myriad of religious doctrines, cults, pseudo-science, and faith-based belief systems that seem to permeate our society today. This ability to imitate, copy, and pass on information provides the opportunity to unleash a replicator that is not based on genes. No other species uses memes as a vehicle to pass on information and ideas.

Charles Darwin, (English naturalist, 1809-1882, father of the theory of evolution) posits, where there is a variation that is advantageous, it will be selected, and passed on to future generations.

So, simple yet so profound! An idea that explains how life can evolve without any kind of design or divine intervention. Evolution is a replicator based on genes. As genes divide they carry this newly selected variation into the next generation. It is gene selection that makes us who we are. The process of gene selection is an endless chain of events, and it reveals to us the arc of evolutionary events that stretch from its beginnings as the division of single cell organisms to all the species on earth. Life on earth took billions of years to evolve into us, and the process continues now and into the future.

SPIRITUALLITY

It is my belief that spirituality comes from within and is an emotional mental state. It is a feeling that one gets when a connection is made that gives a feeling of love and joy. A farmer might feel a spiritual connection to the soil he tills. An artist might feel this while painting or sculpting. One may have this feeling when helping others that might be in distress. Spirituality cannot be found outside the mind and no amount of praying or meditation can give it to you. Spirituality is much older than religious rituals, and probably goes back to our distant ancestors as they felt a oneness with their environment. Spirituality can not only be a religious experience but can expand as a transcendent state that encompasses a search beyond the temporal.

Meditation's goal is to realize who we are. It is described as self-realization. It is said to reveal our emotional and spiritual self. Centering prayer promises much the same results. Any knowledge gained is only a manifestation of the brain and is always a self-centered event. Every experience and every feeling we have ever had is confined to the mind. Why then do we seek spirituality in rituals and exercises outside of the mind? The mind is the beginning and the end of all our experiences.

TRUTH

It would be impossible for us to be aware of everything in our physical world, as well as the cultural and intangible thoughts that make us who we are. In any system or object there are too many nuances and idiosyncrasies for us to grasp. It is through rational and creative thought that we begin to unravel these complexities.

(Friedrich Nietzche)" The most perfidious way of harming a cause consists of defending it deliberately with faulty arguments.'

(Aldous Huxley) "Facts do not cease to exist because they are ignored"

(Gandhi) says "even if you are a minority of one, the truth is the truth."

No one seems to explain what truth is. They all seem to be saying something different. We can only say that truth means different things to different people. There is truth in mathematics, truth in the scientific method, and truth in logic, all of which are subjective. This is the world of the mind. Intuition and faith come from within and are also subjective.

Objective and subjective truth are both self-evident to each individual beholder. We as social beings, living in contact with others must walk a fine line between the two. During the Inquisition it would be unwise to argue against Ptolemy's geocentric universe. Ptolemy's earth centered universe was an advanced theory in this historical time frame, and the Catholic church adopted it as truth. All those who opposed this theory were marked as heretics and were dealt with by the Inquisition. The church opposed Copernicus's theory of a heliocentric universe as blasphemous, to suggest that God's good earth was not the center of the universe. The holy Inquisition lasted approximately 700 years; when the Pope appointed the first inquisitors in 1231 A.D. and ended with the last execution in Spain in 1826.

These views may seem myopic today. We must realize that even thought is an evolutionary process, and today our views are quite different. Our instrumentation and knowledge have allowed us to escape the bondage of the past and extend our reach to the stars.

The greatest truth we can aspire to is to know the whole truth. Theologians tell us that only God knows absolute truth. God, however, does not present himself for queries by men about his existence or the nature of absolute truth. God, it is said, reveals truth to his chosen profits and they in turn give us this revealed word. All this revealed information is referenced in so called sacred books. The laity is told to accept on faith the wisdom of these sacred scriptures. This seems to me to be a roundabout way to find truth, if indeed there is any truth to be found in this way. It is easy to be seduced by the silver-tongued oratory of clerics, priests, and holy men. We must always be on our guard to keep from falling into the trap of being deceived by others.

Most thoughts seem to be relative. Beliefs are products of the mind. Political, ethical, religious and moral beliefs are based on mental considerations, not on the hard-physical world. Truth seems to be subjective. If this is the case, truth is relative. What we hear and believe are only opinions, not necessarily truth.

How do I determine truth? This is what I like to define as functional truth. Simply put it is the best we can know at any given time. It mostly consists of our power to reason, draw logical deductions, and use a little common sense. These deductions must meet the standards of social acceptance if we are to move freely within any given society. Some societies are more tolerant of their citizens than others. If you value your freedom always remember that "big brother" is watching, you. Our thoughts are sovereign and always belong to us, but voice them at your own peril.

(Voltaire 1694-1778) observes, "It is dangerous to be right in matters on which the established authorities are wrong."

QUESTIONING ASSUMPTIONS

An assumption is a presumption that a premise is true. The meaning and value of thoughts and events are derived from basic assumptions. Assumptions constitute a chain of thought that progresses to the fulfillment of a point of view. A point of view is a judgment or an opinion one holds regarding something. Thoughts may be conscious or unconscious, instinctual or learned. The structure of thought and mental activity proceeds from an understanding based on assumptions. It is from the association of ideas formed from assumptions that the mechanisms of thought are engendered. There are many assumptions that are hidden, which we take as truth. They seem to be self-evident and we carry them in our minds. We can never be sure our assumptions are true without careful analysis, and even then, we should keep an open mind. Even with the most careful analysis, new evidence and theories might emerge.

Knowledge, thought, perception, and assumptions along with a myriad of other things are a function of the brain. Our senses are simply connectors that carry information from the outside world to the brain. The brain functions as a self-centered mechanism and controls all we think and do. The brain does not distinguish between reality and illusion, and there is no process or technique we can use that would assure us that our deductions are correct. When we use the scientific method or any other way of deduction to determine reality we can never be sure that we are not just weaving more fantasy illusions from flawed assumptions.

Assumptions were brought into existence when man attempted to interpret objective observable reality, give it a name, and assign to it a personality and property of its own. Observable reality is no more accurate than any other self-grounded reality. We all think in terms of symbols, concepts, inference, and logic, all of which do not act upon real physical objects. The naming of objects and phenomenon are the nuptial bed upon which assumptions are conceived.

If we are to understand the nature of assumptions, we should begin with Nihilism. Nihilism posits that there is no truth or order in the universe, and that all traditional values and morals are meaningless. Nihilism is said to be an encroachment upon reality, and that beliefs are unfounded, and existence is senseless.

(Friedrich Nietzsche, the philosopher who is closely associated with Existentialism and Nihilism) writes, "Every belief is necessarily false because there is simply no true world."

Nihilism destroys reality, and our world view collapses around us. It reduces everything we know to an absolute zero. From this point a new process of thought begins, which leaves behind all the old faith based traditional beliefs, superstitions, and illusions. Nihilism posits that life has no meaning and truth does not exist. If truth does not exist, the statement itself is untrue. This paradox resembles the dog that continually chases his tail only to find that the tail has moved by the time the head arrives.

The philosophy of Nihilism leaves us standing separated and exposed in a world that is foreign and unresponsive to our sensibilities. It was Nietzsche's view that we should develop the strength to face adversity without fleeing into a world of superstition and illusion.

What positive attributes could possibly come from this dearth view of reality? Certainly, new creative processes could reveal themselves. New freedoms that are not shackled by conventional thought might lead us to a new era of understanding. When thought begins at a zero point it might free us from the unfounded baggage we all carry. The one thing Nihilism gives us is permission to question assumptions.

How can we question assumptions? This question must be answered from two points of view. First, we need to examine reality from within the confines of ourselves. This reality is grounded from within and constitutes of a sequence of thought that flows outward from the self. The self is always at the center and is the director and interpreter of all subjective thought. No matter what our senses reveal to us, it is the brain that gives meaning to these subjective realities. The second point of view has its reality based in the objective world of matter, and energy, and its interaction with universal laws. Our senses see the world and send these stimuli to the brain, which processes this information. This allows us to interact in the physical world. It is the self's observation of these objective and subjective worlds, upon which our personal assumptions are founded. These assumptions also contain scripts and memes given to us by others.

When an assumption is made it pushes the truth or illusion along a path which may have no merit or value. To raise the standard of proof required beyond simple assumption can have far reaching consequences for billions of people. If we ask the question, what is the one true religion? we find there is a great deal of diversity. Many people think their religion is the only true one, and all others are living in a fantasy life of delusion.

THE LIBERATED MIND

We can never fully liberate or minds. It would be a good trick if we could. Our limited corporal senses, our flawed memories, and unfounded biases all hold us hostage to the truth. It is the mind that keeps repeating these half-truths, flawed assumptions, and fallacies that prevent us from making informed decisions. We are programed from our earliest childhood to accept these rule of thumb, self-evident, heuristic beliefs, and we use them in our daily lives. We also inherited from our culture all the irrational, and false beliefs that pervade our society. It is difficult to distinguish what is partially true or totally false. Our minds tend to value the beliefs with which we are most familiar, and discount those with attitudes and beliefs different than ours. Our minds look for evidence of what we already believe and ignore any conflicting testimony or proof.

We tend to overestimate antidotal evidence and stories that are unverifiable. The proof of any story or statement rests with the person making the claim. We seldom demand proof, and we either accept it or not. Pseudo-science, and the supernatural, as well as superstition and faith, influence us by their emotional appeal not by logical deduction. The trick is to distinguish between what is true and what we want to believe.

If you truly want to liberate your mind you must be careful what you let into your mind. Do not take emotional responses to ideas and arguments into your mind without considering them rationally. Watch out for frequently accepted fallacies, damaging superstitious absurdities, or things that have no value or importance. This includes any unexamined system or belief. To recognize this is the first most important thing you must do.

Memes that are detrimental to your physical, mental, and moral health are forever trying to find a place in your mind. To keep these damaging memes from your mind is a constant and never-ending chore.

Be aware of the techniques others use to control your mind and thoughts, sometimes called brainwashing.

(Joseph Goebbels, Hitler's propaganda minister) asserts that, "If you tell a lie big enough and keep repeating it, people will eventually come to believe it".

Don't let yourself be caught in any kind of propaganda trap. Political parties, corporations, churches, and cults are particularly adept at these practices. Be careful of motivational meetings and study groups, some may be benign while others may be damaging. Watch out for faith healers, unquestionable sacred truths, clairvoyants, precognition of future events, soothsayers, psychics, telepathy, magic makers, charlatans, hoaxers, extraterrestrials, and things that have no truth or value. If that isn't enough to think about, here are a few other things of no value that can influence your mind, shamans, crackpots, bully's, cranks, mediums, oracles, holy men, prophets, preachers, gurus, mountebanks, and clerics. You might want to be careful of stories, metaphors, proclamations, manifestos, and divine revelations. There is a myriad of other things, people, and places that try to manipulate you into a senseless morass illogical thought.

Deprogramming your mind is a continuous and laborious task. It is not an easy thing to do. Use logic and a healthy dose of skepticism when you encounter anything that asks you to accept on faith, or because someone in authority says so. Do not be manipulated into senselessness and hopeless pursuits. Don't be taken in by an error in cognitive perception. Truth is always on a collision course with unreasoned thinking. Don't be taken in by people trying to sell you something. Remember there is no such thing as a stupid question, only gullible people who do not ask. Consider well the answers you receive. Conclusions are always provisional, and it is acceptable to change your mind in the light of new evidence or better ideas. Always keep your mind flexible and alert. What we think is only what we let into our minds. As computer geeks say, "garbage in garbage out". Memes are continually competing to occupy a place in our minds. We must always be on guard against harmful and meaningless memes that have no value. Truth is sometimes unpleasant and goes against our most cherished ideals. When we give up these ideas we may lose friends and be ostracized from our family and support groups. Your self-confidence and self-respect are two of the most important things that you have, don't let someone steal them from you. There are always people and religious cults trying to capture your mind. Liberating your mind is an arduous task. Always be skeptical, and always think critically.

PART 2

TIME

I will not try to discuss Albert Einstein or Stephen Hawking's theories about time. I will happily leave these theories to those physicists of a greater intellect than mine. This is only a layman's musings about such an erudite subject.

I doubt that any of us will ever, in our life time, travel far or fast enough to experience any meaningful time dilation. We can remember the past, experience the present, and prophesy the future. Time seems to be linear and flows only in one direction. Of these three the present seems the most baffling. The present becomes the past as soon as it arrives, and the future becomes the past as soon as it arrives. Somewhere in between lies the present; and the present is the only existence there is. It is the beginning and the end of existence and all things are contained within its parameters. We are powerless to resist the constraints of the present. Our reality exists only from moment to moment. We only exist in this transitional state between past and future. Is all this just a play on words?

There is also the view taken by some physicists that time does not flow from past to present, but is all located together, and that one moment of time is no more important than any other. This is known as the block theory. To consider one's life in terms of the block theory would be farcical and impossible. Ordinary time seems to facilitate our lives much better.

There is biological or cellular time that regulates the lives of plants and animals. It tells plants when to flower and governs the migratory patterns of birds and animals etc. There is a planetary and a geologic time that is measured in billions of years. It wears down and builds up mountains over eons and gives birth to new stars. These events are evolution in action; and are forever changing the cosmos and the world in which we live.

Man-made time is something quite different. It is man's chimerical idea to make time conform to his view of how things and events should be regulated. Man has compartmentalized time into sections governed by clocks. Most of the civilized world uses these mechanical and digital devices.

Are we just trying to understand that which is unknowable? If we did know, would it solve any of our daily problems? We can reflect on the past plan for the future, but life can only be lived in the present.

(Omar Khayyam, Persian poet and astronomer) writes in his book of quatrains, The Rubaiyat, the following observation.

"The Moving Finger writes; and, having writ, ... Moves on: nor all your piety nor Wit. Shall lure it back to cancel half a line. Nor all your tears wash out a word of it."

HAPPINESS

There is a great deal of diversity between individuals, and no religious, political, or moral life fits all. There are always teachers, sages, and holy men who have the answer to happiness if only you would follow their formula.

It is the search for happiness that directs our behavior, and its activity is sought in many ways. The necessities that sustain life such as food, water, and shelter from the elements merits our utmost attention, as does freedom from pain, anguish, and fear. Your mental attitude toward your fellow man and the world is or course a prime priority. It is our world view that encompasses the degree in which we find our happiness. It is our nature to seek out that which is pleasurable and to avoid that which gives us physical and emotional distress. The mind can know the many things that are said to make us happy, but if you do not experience the emotion of happiness it will elude you and leave you with feelings of discouragement. The long list of things said to bring happiness are useless unless we can find joy in activities and things that are meaningful and have value. Love and joy are the inherent and defining quality of our emotions which serve as a guide to the fulfillment of our quest for happiness.

Our minds are a repository of past events and contain both pleasant and distasteful memories. It is not likely we will find happiness or joy in our lives, if we are distraught, in pain, or our minds constantly dwell on unpleasant and offensive memories. We must learn to cultivate the thoughts and feelings that initialize positive emotions. If we turn our thoughts to the outside, thinking this is where we find happiness, we will discover that the source of happiness is within us. Don't we really create our own happiness?

WHO DO YOU THINK YOU ARE?

In his play, (As you like it, Shakespeare's character Jacques pro-claims) "all the world is a stage and all the men and women merely players".

Jacques philosophical musings on the seven ages of man fall short in trying to explain who we are. It might be easier to answer this question by first asking who we are not. Our name, address, age, occupation, sex, race, education, religion as well as a great number of other facts are just an attempt to classify us into those neat little boxes. Any method used to classify, divide, or pigeonhole us is just another way of separating us from one another. We are not separate things to be put into little boxes. Our identity can only be found in the actions we take for and against the whole range of our contacts with the rest of the world. How can we know who we are without recognizing these relationships? Nothing exists alone everything exists within its environment and every environment exists in an endless network of systems. As much as it irritates our sensibilities nothing is autonomous. Don't we identify ourselves in the way we experience the world? It is the self that does the experiencing and identifies us from other individuals. We also derive our sense of self by our values and convictions, which determines our character and personality.

Socrates said, "the unexamined life is not worth living."

This brings up several interesting questions. Doesn't one need to reach the age of reason before such a judgment can be made? Does the examination of our lives give us more fulfilment? Does ignorance make our lives any less valuable? Is examination any more important than anything else? Isn't life just to be experienced rather than analyzed? If we do not examine our lives we will never know if our lives are worth living. If we wanted to examine our lives where would we start?

Who do you think you are? Do you think you are the master of your fate? Do you recognize yourself as being separate from everything else? Do you think you have freewill? Does dominion over people and things define who you are? Do you think you were created for a purpose? There are no correct answers to these questions. You can think as you please, but thinking does not make it so. The better questions to ask are what leads us to the conclusions about who we are. Are we living in the illusion that we are separate and independent? If this is an illusion, who or what is pulling our strings? It is the plexus of the universe, society, and the interaction and stratification of these different systems that seem to pull us in different directions. Everyone and every institution seem to define who we are, which leaves us with the impossible task of trying to conform to all their ideas. If you try to describe who you are, you will find your definitions seem to fit into those neat little boxes. You know, the ones others use to sort, classify and control your life.

What are you? We are all part of the universe and can never be separated from it. We are biological units made from the elements of the universe. As a species we have evolved genetically into what we are today. Our genetic makeup limits us as a biological unit, and as such we can only act according to our nature. We do not possess any purpose other than the limitations placed on us by our own biology. Everything is determined by natural laws, and man as a product of nature is subject to these same laws. Humans have evolved a consciousness that is unique in that we can project our experiences into the unknown areas of abstract thought. Our minds have evolved to a point that we can entertain transcendental thought, cosmic awareness, and even mystical experiences. However, we can never escape the bonds of our biology. Doesn't our biology marry us to the physical world? We should concentrate on our unity with nature in all its configurations and physiognomy. Doesn't social order have its basis in our own psychological and biological needs?

THE SOUL, SELF, AND THE EGO

What a perplexing and enigmatic trio this is. Each seems to be a separate concept, yet they seem interconnected. When you try to describe them from any of their distinguishing parts of religion, philosophy, or psychology they all seem to loosely coalesce around the same center. This is only natural because they are all products of the mind and not of the physical world.

The soul is thought to be immaterial or spiritual in concept. It is also thought to be the life force. It is the essence of the moral and emotional nature of the individual. The soul can be likened to a thought. We know that thoughts exist, but they are expressions of the mind and cannot be measured. If you are religious or spiritual and have faith, there is no conflict. You know that the soul exists and that it is the part of you that passes into another plain of existence. It is the entity that survives death and receives divine judgment on the life lived. The soul is either given eternal salvation or damnation in accordance with divine judgment. In some religions judgment is rendered some place in-between.

The self is a combination of emotions and sensations that merge together to constitute, establish, and identify the totality of the individual. The self is the quality that is thought to identify our consciousness from that of other beings. The body and mind are the container of these emotions and sensations. Together they constitute the self. The self reflects consciousness and is the subject and initiator of one's own actions. It is thought to be by some religions and spiritual sects to be the vessel which harbors the soul. The self is an evolving entity and is an independent and self-contained existence of the body and mind. Everything we learn as we evolve is contained somewhere in the neural network, which is the vast storage place of the knowledge, thoughts, sensations and experiences we draw upon as we go about our daily lives. As we mature from infancy to adulthood and into old age the self's awareness also evolves. When the brain dies the self loses its identity.

The ego is the arbitrator between the individual and the physical world. It functions in our perception of reality, and the way we react and adapt to the world around us. The ego gives us the sense that we are separate and unique from everything else. We seem to be the center of our own actions and feelings. This is the very essence of the ego. The ego by its very nature has an exaggerated view of its own self-importance. The ego turns our thoughts inward and functions as an action and thought device with the self at the center. The ego constantly reinvents itself to strengthen the facade it presents to the outside world. The ego is always reaching for more power and prestige. The ego is an accumulator of things. It is always seeking more control and must continually buttress itself against criticism as it tries to maintain its own self-importance. The ego thrives on its own arrogance, pride, vanity, hubris and conceit.

The ego is not who we are but marries us to a false identity which separates us from our place in the universe. We can only overcome this sense of false identity when we realize that we are not separate, but only a part of all existence. This realization does not transcend the ego. The ego is ever present and only serves as the mediator between the self and the accommodation of our reality. Meditation and self-discipline can't free us from the ego. These techniques may be useful to experience some personally perceived spiritual truth. These practices only serve the ego on a higher and more personal level. This part of our psyche is ever present and reinforces the illusion that we are separate.

We are a part of all that is and each and everything is its own center. Everything in the universe has its own center and resonates harmoniously around the whole. There is no independence, and the ego is only an illusion. The ego requires a relationship with the other for its existence. One cannot swim without water. One cannot walk without gravity to hold us to the earth. Light and darkness, sound and silence cannot be known without the other. One cannot breathe without air. As we take air into our lungs it becomes a part of us, and as we exhale it becomes a part of something else. It is the interaction of everything that constitutes the whole. Nothing stands alone. Everything exists simultaneously in an undiminished union with the whole universe. Subject and background cannot be separated. Separateness is just an illusion. We cannot know anything without recognizing and considering its opposing factors. It is the exclusion of opposites that is the mother of intolerance. We must learn to recognize the existence of diverse opinions, and that they will always exist. Once we accept and reconcile this fact we will have learned the meaning of tolerance.

Our senses seem to allow us to experience the world as separate parts, but we only experience an extension of ourselves. This exposes the ego as an illusion and that the self is not separate. We all exist in and as an inseparable part of all existence. Some people believe that this realization is the beginning of wisdom. When one divides the person into two separate parts, the spiritual and the physical the two halves alienate each other by their perception of separation. This perception cannot be resolved because there is no separation. Why then do we cling to the delusion of separateness?

MORALITY

Morality is conformity to the ideals of human conduct and is a set of tools we use to determine right from wrong. Animals have little or no morality they only act and react in accordance with their genes. If we had no reference to our culture, philosophy, or religious foundations, we would have no basis for morality. Does morality regulate behavior? Many people think that morals are a divine gift from God. Others might argue that morals are based on the principals of humanity and utility. Regardless of the origins of morals they are beneficial to all those who wish to live in peace and tranquility within a society. Ethics create a guide and set of rules for use by stable societies and each society determines how to regulate and control behavior by their laws. Many laws are neither right nor moral but only reflect the preferences of those who have the power to enact and enforce them. Some laws are good and well-intended, and they serve the people with justice and without prejudice; others only give the appearance of virtue. What seems to have meaning or purpose is only a reflection of our values. Any system of ethical behavior is most often a mixture of ideas and confused examples from many diverse sources. Those who do not apply reason to their ideologies might find their moral values to be hypocritical or paradoxical. It is important to know how and why you reached your conclusions. If you let others think for you, you only become a pawn in promulgating their ideas. Each one of us is the final judge of the merits of our own thoughts and actions.

Albert Einstein writes "the foundations of morality should not be made dependent on myth nor tied to any authority least doubt about the myth or the legitimacy of the authority imperial the foundation of sound judgment and action."

It was the interpretation of morality that ended free inquiry and substituted faith as a moral code. It ended a thousand years of enlightenment and substituted a fixed theology that embarked upon all manner of atrocities. These indiscretions were committed under the sanctions of the church. This unfortunate period of religious rule was known as the Inquisition. Few of us today would hold these myopic expressions of faith. However, there are those whose faith allows ethnic cleansing, the execution of infidels, or the condemnation to hell of those who do not share their point of view. This expression of faith has done irrevocable damage to clear and logical thought because it masquerades as ethical truth.

Clerics, priests, politicians, and all manor or other persons and organizations would deny you the privilege of thinking for yourself. They want you to accept their dogmas, creeds, and ideas on faith. This seems to give the illusion of freewill and leads us to accept the illogical and chimerical as truth. This pattern of thought steals away our most precious possession, the capacity to think for ourselves. Freedom of thought allows us to think for ourselves and to accept the logical and discount the illogical. Most of all it gives us the ability to change our mind in the light of new evidence and knowledge. This allows us to grow and mature rather than to be incarcerated by faith, meaningless rituals, and dogmas. The more time and effort we put into something, the more it becomes a part of our lives and the less likely we are to surrender it to change. It is like trying to lose weight or break a bad habit.

The most grievous and insidious of these indoctrinations is to manipulate and control the impressionable minds of young people.

You don't have to look far to see the examples and relationships of this kind of indoctrination. Young people trained as suicide bombers, are taught to rebel against infidels, to keep their women in bondage and stone adulterers. Others are taught racism, ethnic cleansing, bigotry, and engage in purging society of homosexuals, flag burners, and other forms of preconceived wickedness. They would deny you the right to read anything they might find to be objectionable. These people believe the world is full of devils and evil doers bent on destroying their righteous and virtuous tranquility. Young people are enlisted to give up their freedom and their lives to preserve these toxic ideas.

From the mid to late 1930's I was sent to live with my grandparents who resided in a small town in east Texas. Many of the people there, like those in this region of the country were fundamentalist evangelical Christians. They went to church every Sunday. They went to prayer meetings, Bible study, and did their best to walk in the paths of righteousness. They filled their days with endless devotion to the Almighty. The Good Book was always the last word for it was the word of God and was never to be questioned. Everyone quoted scripture, praised the wisdom of Solomon, and dammed the sins of Cain. It was in this environment that I was introduced to the nature of the Almighty God. Almighty God as he was always referred to was all knowing, all seeing and all powerful. This omnipotent God had given to us strict laws of thought and behavior. The penalty for the transgression of these laws was too dreadful to contemplate. The terrifying visions of pain, agony, and hellfire filled my impressionable young mind with these dreadful apparitions of divine justice. Every bad thought that crept into my mind I knew would displease God, and I would suffer in perdition's eternal lake of fire. I would be tormented by devils for even the most trivial of peccadilloes. I feared falling asleep at night, afraid that demons would carry me away to some dreadful and loathsome place of eternal atonement. There was no place to hide and no thought could be concealed from that all-seeing eye and all-knowing intellect. To displease God was to invite everlasting damnation.

Every child and every human being need a place free from the wrath of an omnipotent and vengeful God. We need a place to think as we please and to vent our frustrations without the repercussions of divine justice. In my view there is no greater sin than to hold the intellect in this bondage of ignorance.

We all live by our own personal morality and no one can speak for us or decide what is moral for us and what is not. Don't we all act in such a way as to bring us the most happiness and that kind of life we wish to live? It is through self-understanding and the interactions with the rest of the world that we build our own code of conduct and morals.

FAITH

Faith might be defined as trust and believing in something for which there is no proof. Faith is a tool and a vehicle used to understand reality in a world where knowledge is claimed without proof or logic. Faith makes objective claims about the workings of the natural world from the products of personal priority, not from scientific or logical thought. Religious faith is belief in the traditional doctrines, and the principle systems of its creed. It is the complete trust and devotion to these doctrines that give to God unquestionable fealty. In many religions, belief and faith are considered virtues, no matter how ludicrous or chimerical the claim. To them these claims seem perfectly natural, after-all who can know the mind of God? We have no self-correcting mechanism to recognize or identify truth.

The Nicene Creed, or the Apostles' Creed, except for a few word changes and used in different ways is the affirmation of faith of most Christian churches. This is an edited copy of an original text, which is its own authority.

"I believe in God, the Father almighty, creator of heaven and earth. I believe in Jesus Christ, his only son, our Lord, who was conceived by the Holy Spirit, born of the Virgin Mary, suffered under Pontius Pilate, was crucified, died, and was buried;

he descended to the dead. On the third day, he rose
again; he ascended into heaven, he is seated at the
right hand of the Father, and he will come to judge
the living and the dead." (The Catholic Church
has added the following.) "I believe in the Holy
Spirit, the holy Catholic Church, the communion
of saints, the forgiveness if sins, the resurrection of
the body, and life everlasting. Amen."

Only faith and belief can give it any convincing acceptance.
Science and reason give no determination of its degree of validity.
When faith is added to the equation, it can destroy the credibility of
anything it wishes, if people have faith in it. Belief in the scientific
method and proven heuristic practices are of great benefit in the
orderly reasoning of the mind.

(Pope Gregory 1 540- 604) "Faith has no merit where reason
supplies the truth."

Superstition and outlandish claims should be dismissed without verifiable evidence to back such assertions. The promise of
everlasting life after death, and the expectation of justice in heaven,
cheapens the life we live here on earth. Faith disappoints the intellect and undermines our understanding of reality. We all live in the
real world, which is devoid of unquestionable truths, and claims, or
some order of existence beyond reason.

The scientific method, reason, and observation do not serve
us well when we try to analyze such things as values and morals.
These subjects are best left for your personal preferences. Critical
thinking and science embraces the methods for testing things in
this world, philosophy is best used to determine issues of ethics.
Faith has no bearing on the validity of divinity, and belief does not
change reality.

Holy wars are characteristically faith-based or religious in
nature. They are brought about when religious ideology is the

motivating force. The term "Holy War" is a the credibility contradiction or an oxymoron. No war can be considered holy that kills innocent people, obliterates property, and destroys a state tranquility. Many so called Holy Wars are waged under a false flag to hide the greed and grievances of monarchs and other sovereign rulers. We should be very careful to accept any motive to go to war. Those who allow themselves to be used as pawns in such conflicts are mindless drones, only to be discorded when the conflict is over.

END-TIME & SECOND COMING

End-time, Last Days, End of Days or by whatever name you choose to call it, is the doctrine of the Apocalypse of John. The author is said to be *(John of Patmos about 81 AD)*. Groups of fundamentalist Christians have looked to these bizarre prophecies for the signs of the End-Times described in the book of Revelation. True believers of every age have tried to interpret these prophecies and link them to current events of political, social, and environmental upheaval. They are trying to link these prophecies in a sequence of events to the second coming of Christ. These apocalyptic visions have beguiled millions of true believers into these extraordinary predictions of the Bible. Those who take these writings as literal truth are unwavering in their convictions and sincerity. They would shape world events to facilitate the End-Time prophecies, regardless of the consequences. They are causing irrefutable damage to the environment and eco-system. Their position is that we need not care for the environment because the End-Times are near at hand. There will be no need for clean water or air as we enter God's kingdom.

These fundamentalist sects feel that the future of the planet is of no relevance, and good stewardship is not germane or timely. They think that the destruction of the planet and the environment are the antecedent of a joyful event. It is a sign that the apocalypse is near at hand, and we are living in the End-Times when Christ will return. The sinners will be cast into hellfire, and the righteous, living and dead will be taken into heaven. This event is known as the rapture, and all the non-believers will be left behind to endure seven years of great suffering. These adverse events will give rise to the Antichrist and the battle of Armageddon and are known as the Tribulation. The Tribulation will usher in the four horsemen to spread war, famine, pestilence, and death. When these events come to pass the time of redemption is near and God will reign supreme.

This extreme and exclusive world view is one of the basic elements of the fundamentalist Christian faith. It is their intent to promulgate and force this ideology upon the whole of society. Fundamentalists through cunning manipulation, and misrepresentation, have infiltrated every aspect of government and society. They would hasten the countdown and pave the way for the second coming of Christ.

Our nation's largest polluters are happy to support candidates of this mindset, as it is in their best economic interest to do so. They supply enormous sums of money to buy candidates who support their agendas. The paradigm of this extreme fundamentalist group is to convert the nation into a theocracy-based system which dictates prayer, and evangelical Christian values. Any theocracy-based system of government which gives its allegiance to God cannot be a true democracy. The very essence of democracy is derived in the will of the people it serves, not by any interpretation of God's will by religious leaders.

Religious cults abound, offering enlightenment and everlasting life. What could be a more enticing offer than everlasting life and enlightenment? All you must do is follow a few simple rules and live your life according to the scriptures in the holy book. The belief in life after death lessens the value of the life we live here and now. These controlling cults restrict thoughts with destructive brain washing techniques. Charismatic people persuade others to follow their ideas, often to their own detriment.

Jim Jones founded the People's Temple and led his people to Guiana to find a new life. Some people wanted to leave the cult.

When congressman Leo Ryan came to investigate, he was set upon by thugs, and was murdered as he was about to fly back to the United States. Jones, because of his own paranoia, persuaded his followers to drink Kool Aid laced with cyanide. Those who rebelled were murdered, and a total of 909 people lost their lives because of the orders of this cult leader.

David Korech led the Branch Davidians, a religious sect of the Seventh-day Adventist church, to a fiery death at Waco Texas. The initial standoff left 4 ATF agents and 7 Davidians dead. The FBI ended the siege with the burning of the center. David Korech and 79 others were found dead.

Marshall Applewhite and the followers of Heaven's Gate took their own lives. They believed a flying saucer hiding behind the Comet Hale-Bopp would take them to heaven. There were 39 members who died in this senseless act.

These are dangerous cults that poison the mind and spread hate and prejudice between their followers and others. Many of these cults are subtle and highly skillful in their manipulation to bring new followers into their group. It seems every religion and every organization have its lunatic fringe. These people are hopelessly and irretrievably lost in a morass of illogical dogma. They present a danger to clear and logical thought because they would force their agendas on the rest of the world. These fallacious and invalid ideas have led to wars and the destruction of the environment. All this in the name of holy predestination.

Extremists constitute only a small part of the world's religions. Most people believe in the preservation of the planet and its biological diversity. They want to keep the earth, skies, and waters clean and safe for themselves and their children. They are willing to share earth's bounty and live in peace and harmony with their neighbors. Many are aware of the abuses of power that occur in the absence of the separation of church and state. Most people are tolerant and respectful of other people's beliefs and opinions.

DOGMAS AND RITUALS

Dogma has as its foundation, axioms and concepts which are thought to be indisputable, self-evident, and fundamental. It is upon these foundations that most religions base their core values.

The theology of any religion is a set of established opinions held in common by the members of that specific creed. These opinions constitute a doctrine of morals and faith that set the boundaries, principles, and philosophies of that group. It is these indisputable values that are expanded upon that create dogma. If the core values of their hypothesis and basic assumptions are incorrect, the beliefs that are derived from them are also incorrect. Those who embrace these values are living lives of self-deception. It is hard to fault a person for their credulity when they were conditioned from childhood to believe and have faith in superstitious and erroneous instruction.

Examples, such as astrology, believe the alignment of the planets and other celestial bodies have an influence on their personal lives and world events. The position and movement of these celestial bodies are charted and given reference in the horoscope. Astrologers interpret these positions to calculate their importance in worldly events, as well as our daily lives. Other practices seek to foretell future events by the aid of special knowledge, or the supernatural powers of divination. The readings of tea leaves, Ouija boards, tarot cards, and the like, also have their followers. The people who promote these crafts are said to be charlatans, and their crafts are known as pseudoscience. These practices are generally regarded by their followers as mystical truth. The same could be said of more orthodox religions that base their dogmas on faith and unprovable facts. Dogma is a vehicle used to spread incorrect interpretations in a never-ending perpetual cycle of erroneous information. This misdirected information is communicated within the population of those who adhere to these fundamental self-evident truths. These dogmas and indisputable truths are accepted on faith, not scientific or rational examination. Dogma demands that you accept these assumptions and presuppositions as truth.

Be very careful what you let into your mind. The world is full of people and organizations fighting to control your mind and thoughts. If the major premise is wrong, it logically follows that its reality is also flawed. Avoid dogma and doctrines that close the mind to the truth of logic and science. Destructive memes are always competing for a place in your mind. You are the gatekeeper of your own mind. Don't be led into a state of disordered thinking.

Rituals are acts that are promulgated by the traditional rules of specific organizations. Their purpose is to strengthen and give credence to their dogmas. Ritual acts take on a variety of forms, such as reciting specific prayers in special sequences, chanting, and the singing of hymns. These acts give the group a feeling of cohesiveness. Bowing, kneeling, and genuflection are ritual acts of submission, obedience, and reverence. Sermons are also ritual acts that instruct and inform the laity of the proper moral and political correctness their lives should reflect.

Many rituals take on bazaar behavior such as self-mutilation, snake handling, fire-walking, symbolic cannibalism, and speaking in tongues, to name just a few. Faith healing is a dangerous and risky practice. I personally know of a couple who were Christian Scientists and their religion believed God would heal their sick child. Prayer was substituted for medical attention and the child died. Another such incident occurred when a child was bitten by a rattlesnake. The child was given a prayer and sent to bed without medical attention. This child also died. This kind of faith can have disastrous results.

Organized religion distances its followers from their inherent place in the universe, by focusing conscious attention on ritual. The reinforcement of church doctrine is what ritual is all about. Ritual directs the mind away from logical thought and steals our sense of oneness with the universe. Fundamentalist rituals that interpret divine laws, and revealed word, attempt to seduce followers to distinguish and distance themselves from other points of view and belief systems. Many psychological and social problems occur when we make unwise choices or try to follow flawed assumptions. The more one adheres to these doctrines and rituals, the narrower their perspective becomes. Doesn't the answer lie in education rather than indoctrination? Shouldn't we focus our thoughts outward to encompass a universal awareness?

PSEUDO-SCIENCE AND OTHER NONSCIENCE

Here are a few examples that clutter the mind with useless pursuits, astrology, intelligent design, crop circles, extrasensory perception (ESP), full moon lunacy, channeling, remote viewing, clairvoyance, telepathy, spiritualism, biorhythms, numerology, perpetual motion, levitation, alien abductions, faith healing, q-rays, homeopathy, magnetic therapy, chelation therapy, dianetics, parapsychology, phrenology, feng-shui, exobiology, cold fusion, hollow-earth, flat-earth, fairies, elves, leprechauns, unicorns, ghosts, shape-shifters, goblins, gnomes, devils, vampires, warewolves, gods & angels.

There are so many conspiracy theories I can't begin to name them. Do you believe in Big Foot, the Jersey Devil, or the Mothman? How about Atlantis, The Bermuda Triangle, El Dorado, or Shangri La?

There is a myriad of other beliefs, prejudices, biases, and superstitions, that cloud our logical thinking. They guide us on a course toward false convictions that have no value.

PART 3

RATIONALISM

(René Descartes 1595-1650 father of modern western philosophy)

Descartes offers a worldview that concerns itself with the affairs of this world. One that is not monastic or ecclesiastical. It is the philosophy of Rationalism, as it deals with the matters of this world rather than other worldly concepts. Rationalism is a concept and attitude that encompasses reason and sensibility. It rejects that which is absurd, fallacious, and cannot be tested by reason. It doubts the truth of divine revelation and never accepts anything based on faith.

There is nothing in Rationalism that is ever exempt from examination, experimentation, or inquiry. Nothing can remain the exclusive possession of anyone or any organization claiming special knowledge, or privilege. Rationalism is a battle for the conquest of one's own mind against the ubiquitous onslaught of irrational thought that permeates all of society. When our minds are free we can move into unknown areas of understanding, without prejudice. Rationalism provides a pathway for social and philosophical examination outside of religious or supernatural beliefs.

Rationalism is one-way humankind can effectively challenge things that seem to be beyond our knowledge and imagination. There will always be unknown challenges in the pursuit of unraveling the mysteries of the universe, and of ourselves. Rationalism is a tool by which we can critically analyze the beliefs of cults, religions, political, and philosophical ideologies. Rationalism exposes dogmas and rituals to the light of intelligent reasoning. Rationalism holds no doctrine or formal creed but brings an intellectual approach to religion. Rationalists dismiss the miracles of the bible and embrace the inherent goodness of mankind. There are no answers offered by Rationalism as to how or when the universe was created, who created it, or what happens to us after death. These questions seem to be beyond our comprehension. Religion, however seems to have numerous explanations for these events, most of which are super-natural. There are always saviors and messiahs ready to give you the answers to life's most perplexing questions. All you need is faith in their doctrines and explanations. There seems to be no credible evidence for the existence of God, nor can it be proved that God does not exist. Any evidence one way or the other is inconclusive. In the absence of any definitive evidence it would be prudent just to admit that we simply do not know and proclaim ourselves to be Agnostics. Perhaps we should all be Agnostic about things for which there is no credible evidence. Most Rationalists embrace their philosophy out of choice, not out of ignorance, or what they were conditioned to believe from early childhood. What is it that brings Atheists and Agnostics together to do good deeds, and help others? It is the same thing that binds the people of religious persuasion together, their inherent belief that we are all human and should exhibit compassion, love, forgiveness, tolerance, and self-discipline. If we do not express these qualities, we might find ourselves to be less than human.

When faced with so many conflicting religious philosophies, and ideas, it is easy to fall into a state of confusion. It is obvious that they can't all be true. It is easy to be persuaded by false assumptions if we do not think through these ideas as a viable concept of rational understanding. Reality is an understanding based on the structure of critical reasoning, and logical thought.

REALITY DISTORTIONS

There is an insidious distortion that permeates our daily lives, it rips apart the strands of reality, and replaces it with the influences of the powered oligarchy. Their identity separates them from the people that constitute the masses. They masquerade as the servants of society; however, it is society that serves them. They define the moral code, and the political correctness of our actions. They are the captains of industry, the law givers, defenders of the faith, and the enforcers. They attempt to create a singularity of thought and reaction to their ideologies and icons. They wish to control your choices, beliefs, thoughts, and actions. They set the agendas that select and control our perception of reality. It is their visions that shape and govern our society. Big money dominates the economy, cultural, and political life of our country. Their tools are media, government, the military complex, religious sects, corporations, law enforcement, front organizations, unions, economic and educational institutions, to name just a few. Freedom of thought is limited through censorship and the manipulation of propaganda. The use of television, radio, cinema, magazines, and books are but a few vehicles by which propaganda is used to persuade us. Their scripted visions and voices of authority distort our perception of reality. They divide us from our humanity and substitute meaningless and destructive ideas, notions, and scintillating generalities.

Our only recourse is to substitute logic and reason for the repetitious onslaught of these ideas.

Our minds are always free to think as we please, but we are never free from the continuous invasion of these thoughts and visions. We possess an automatic and unconscious mind that has little will of its own. It reacts in accordance with our beliefs and assumptions. There are always icons, slogans, and destructive memes that strengthen their grip on our subconscious minds. They seem to escape the notice of our conscious minds, as they indoctrinate us to work their will. It is only through rational thought that we can change our reactions and bring them into the focus of conscious awareness. We should ask ourselves if there is any rational reason to accommodate such beliefs. If not, is it prudent to continue to harbor them?

Freedom of thought can be smothered and repressed by using language, and redefining words into language that is politically correct. The Views of the indoctrinated majority suppress dissenting opinions and freedom of thought. The same can be said of a loud and vocal minority. Freedom of thought is the freedom of any individual to hold a viewpoint regardless of anyone else's opinion.

The omission of facts, distortion, misdirection, and outright lies, are used by the powered gentry to capture your thoughts and persuade you to their will. It is their intention to keep the people in a state of stupefaction. These powered elite have no loyalty to their employees or the consumers of their products and services. They have little interest in the welfare of humanity, or the ecology of the planet. Their only concern is to perpetuate their myths and smother free thought. They are identified by their greed and arrogance.

Each of these entities have enormous executive power. They are intertwined and affect the political, cultural, and economic activities of society. There is government intervention in corporate activities, and the military, and they in turn bring pressure to bear on the affairs of state. We as ordinary citizens, are only vaguely aware that something beyond our control is shaping our daily lives. There is something that directs us to work on projects in which we have no voice. Large corporations have bought or run out of business smaller competitors. They consolidate power into virtual monopolies, and as consumers we are left with little choice, either buy or do without.

I do not infer that all people of privilege are among the ruling class; some known as the idle rich are content to live their lives in their own social class, indifferent and ignorant of the lives of those who service them. Their frame of reference does not include the lower and middle classes; they think they were created only to serve them. These cavalier attitudes distant them from reality. Others are great benefactors and humanitarians. Rational people know the difference.

This powerful oligarchy finances and directs the organizations and institutions that have a special interest in protecting, enhancing, and maintaining their position of power, wealth, and social privilege. Their engagement in corporate structures, their friends, education, and their personal interests, identify them with the power elite. Their power is centrated in their command of institutional hierarchies. It is their intent to persuade the masses to act on their behalf and perpetrate their elite status. Politicians make the laws that protect these entities. It is the duty of the police and military to enforce these laws. These institutions coalesce into the forces that shape societies. The individual and family units are all but powerless to initiate any kind of change.

Most people want to live in a clean, safe, and healthy environment. Corporations want to do business as usual and do whatever it takes for their financial gain. The cleanup of polluting byproducts cut into corporate profits and are not cost effective. The degradation of the eco-system upsets the balance of nature. The people seem powerless to avert the inevitable consequences of this global onslaught on the environment.

We spend most of our waking hours servicing the corporations for which we work, bending to their demands while trying to maintain our own economic needs. What little time we have for entertainment and activities of our choosing is continuously inundated with advertisements and corporate propaganda. We are subject to the laws and restraints of our communities, as well as the faith and morality of our religious institutions. Our schools teach young people to conform to the disciplines that will serve the needs of the industrial complex and the society that depends upon it. These institutions have altered our lives and the way we experience the physical and mental qualities that make up our existence. These ideas and dogmas dominate our lives; and we are only partly aware of their influence. Discrimination against labor, by legislative means, strike breaking practices, outsourcing of jobs, and a minimum wage, have been a wanton and willful assault on the working class. These practices and laws dictate the value of labor. Working class persons have little recourse to set the value of their labor. Labor is the backbone that supports the whole of society; without labor, there would be no vehicle to move the economy. Without labor, there would be no services, no products to buy, or means of manufacture.

The privileged few are determined to impose and create upon the people a new world order over which only the privileged few will rule. These attitudes are the antecedent of a dangerous downward spiral of the middle class, and white-collar workers. If these attitudes prevail we will be falling into a never-ending slide into poverty. Many of the world's people are now living on the edge of the abyss. Only abject poverty, and hopelessness of spirit awaits them.

Pope Francis (Leader of the Catholic Church) says "Money has to serve, not to rule. We have created new idols, the golden calf of old has found a new and heartless image in the cult of money and the dictatorship of an economy which is faceless and lacking any truly human goal. A new invisible and at times virtual, tyranny is established, one which unilaterally imposes its own laws and rules."

PROPAGANDA

Propaganda is the spreading of ideas and opinions in support of a cause; it is used to manipulate the mind and emotions and persuade you to accept a point of view. These methods are most often used by commercial, political, and religious entities. It is important to recognize the different techniques used as the vehicles to maneuver your thoughts, often against your best self-interest.

Words that are general in nature and cannot be proven like fair and balanced, reliable, honest and good, are often used to cloak the truth. These words when used to deceive are specious and disingenuous. They are an attempt to sway opinion because their connotation suggests they are free from deception or fraud.

There are examples of using a country's flag, color guard, or persons of high rank, to make their point seem patriotic. The use of holy symbols, relics, and scripture from holy books, make one's words seem righteous. They give the speaker an air of integrity. Listen carefully to detect hypocrisy, and faulty logic.

Name calling is used to discredit someone or some idea by giving it a negative label. Degenerate, sinful, greedy, lustful, and a host of other remarks are used to cast aspersions on an opponent rather than talk about issues. These pejorative remarks might refer to an individual as a card-carrying member of a group they wish to besmirch. These words generally express only an assertion. The listener is left to provide their own interpretation.

Evading the issue by changing the subject is used when a speaker wishes to avoid a topic.

Faulty logic is used when comparing two similar things that have little in common with the other. Apples and oranges are both fruits, but their characteristics are quite different.

Contradictory statements within the same argument are another use of faulty logic.

The presentation of facts that support only one side, and deliberately omit facts or information that may be pertinent to understanding an issue is a ruse that is often used.

Guilt by association is used to slander one's reputation, by presenting them as members of a satanic cult, their association with felons, or persons of dubious character.

There is an abundance of other forms of propaganda; they all seek to persuade you to their point of view. It would serve the reader well to beware of what you let into your mind. The consequences can be devastating or have no credence. You might well be entertaining defective reasoning. Everything we hear is surfeited with someone else's propaganda.

Joseph Goebbels (Hitler's propaganda minister from 1939 to1945) "If you tell a lie big enough and keep repeating It, people will eventually come to believe it. The lie can be maintained only for such time as the state can shield the people from the political, economic and /or military consequences of the lie. It thus becomes vitally important for the state to use all its powers to repress dissent, for the truth is the mortal enemy of the lie, and thus by extension the truth is the greatest enemy of the state."

WAGE-SLAVERY

Today wage-slavery is a form of oppression used by capitalists to make workers totally dependent on income from their labor. We no longer labor under the whip of a slave master or a feudal land owner. We have finally rid ourselves of chattel and bond slavery, but we now find ourselves to be in the servitude of the capitalist. Workers must now acquiesce to the authority of an employer. Even the most basic human needs can be withheld reducing one to oppressive destitution. Slave-wages are better suited to the employer than chattel slavery. There is no need for food, housing, or a variety of other human services. The old, sick, and superfluous workers are simply made redundant. To maintain any degree of solvency workers must put their labor at the disposal of the capitalist. The hash penalty for not working is impoverishment and being deprived of any means of existence.

Owner Capitalists and wage earners each have their own agendas. Wage earners want to earn enough to take care of their families and achieve some degree of upward mobility. They want to be able to purchase the necessities of life and give to their children a better chance in life. The Capitalists want to grow their capitol and expand their sphere of influence. They want to buy labor at the lowest possible cost to maximize profits. These contradictory views place them on opposite sides of a never-ending conflict. It is this division that fosters social stratification and is the wellspring of most class conflict. Mobility between classes is rare.

It seems we never get ahead. The myth persists that if we work hard, and if we are loyal to our employers we will be rewarded with advancement, privilege, and job security. We are told that we can live the American dream if only we would play by their rules. Nothing could be further from the truth. The asymmetry between the wealthy, the poor, and the middle class is a huge chasm and growing every day. Your loyalty is rewarded with downsizing, or your job moved to a foreign country. It is not unusual to train your lower wage replacement, before having your job terminated. More and more workers find longer hours and harsher working conditions as they find themselves without labor unions to defend them. The people have been hoodwinked into believing that the status quo is the best way to order society. To question its principals is subversive and an attack on the fundamental American way of life. Capitalism has only replaced earlier forms of oppression. What freedoms we have, has been won by the long and difficult struggle of the working class. You do not have to be an economic expert to see the rich on one side and the declining wages on the other. Simple arithmetic is sufficient to see that the wealthy ruling class has taken its wealth by emptying the pockets of ordinary citizens.

The easy use of credit cards has become common place, and the people who habitually use them pay a heavy price. They become economic slaves to the credit industry; and their only purpose is to continuously service the debt. With late fees, minimum payments, and other hidden fees your credit card debt could expand to an untenable rate. If the average citizen used the same tactics as the credit industry it would be called loan sharking.

Illegal aliens are individuals who enter a country in violation of that country's laws. Most come to escape grinding poverty, and to find a better life for their families, many of them seek safety from oppressive governments and marauding bands of thugs.

Corporations have lured them here with promises of opportunity and advancement. They find neither, but only slave-wages and a life of drudgery. Corporations use their labor only to increase the ratio of their profit, which seems to be their end game. These inequitable living conditions have driven illegal aliens to secure benefits such as health care, welfare, and free public education. This staggering influx has placed a great burden on our already strained socio-economic system. It is left for the middle class to pick up cost of services. Corporations pay little or nothing. Our elected representatives do not acknowledge or seem to be willing to correct this imbalance.

Most countries have laws against hiring illegal immigrants. However, the penalties are rarely enforced allowing employers to thumb their noses at these laws. Illegal immigrants can be found in jobs that pay substandard wages. American workers are losing their jobs to illegal immigrants, and corporations are replacing workers by sending their jobs overseas to be filled by cheap foreign labor. Illegal immigrants fill jobs that cannot be sent overseas because their location and requirements are local.

CLASS CONFLICT

It is little wonder that class conflict permeates all strata of social interaction. This conflict takes many forms. It begins in the family with the father, mother, and usually with the birth order of the siblings. It progresses to the schoolyard, and extends to the workplace. It culminates in the board room, and with a small group of individuals who exercise control over every of aspect of our lives. Class conflict is a game of one-upmanship, of power, privilege, and dominance. It is an activity in which the ego shows its true colors. Conflict can be as benign as sibling rivalry, or it can rip apart the fabric of society with bloody revolution. It can be found in every guise through which it moves. Culture, religion, education, race, and gender all play their part in creating inequality. Consolidated wealth contributes to this inequity and manifests itself in the adversarial relationship between capital and labor.

Political influence directed by the industrial and manufacturing base is self-evident. Politicians in their own self-interest serve the oligarchy of the ruling class and the moneyed elite.

Modern society embraces a vast display of cultural ideals and special interest groups, each of which have their own agendas. Each group has its own specific hierarchy be it secret society, political party, labor union, or religious institution. The division of labor is essential in every society. If everyone had to do for one's self, and not rely on the knowledge and skill of others, we would probably not have survived as a species. The separation of class survives today as it did in feudal societies with wealth and power concentrated in the hands of the few. The capitalist pays as little as possible and lets the worker struggle to maintain his own existence. If everyone were treated fairly and equally, and if we could work together to eliminate adversarial attitudes, we could come much closer to living in a utopian society. It is man's inhumanity that is the fountainhead of hopelessness and despair.

Any discussion of class conflict would be incomplete without a mention of the doctrines of Karl Marx.

(Karl Marx 1818-1883 philosopher, economist and revolutionary socialist) In his critique Das Kapital Marks deals with capitalism and the market economy.

Marx thought that Capitalism would fail unless the system adopted "universal suffrage". The masses of disenfranchised workers should put aside their differences and out vote those who serve the moneyed elite. Marx thought that capitalism contained the seeds of its own destruction. Marx was not a Leninist or a Stalinist, but was a social scientist, and developed a socialist system that has been used as a model around the world. Marx was a believer in the rights, wisdom, and virtue of the common people. Marx realized that any real democracy rests in the sovereignty of the people. Only a political party that truly serves the people can be a true democracy.

Many Communist and Socialist states did not follow Marxist ideals but became totalitarian in nature. The revolutions that followed, spawned a new class of society, as old masters were expelled and traded for new. The common people just ended up serving the new masters. Communism and Capitalism have both failed to serve the people in any meaningful way.

SURVEILLANCE & INCARCERATION

Is "big brother" watching you? You bet he is! Surveillance cameras are being placed everywhere imaginable, and in some places you would never imagine. Employers use them, and a variety of other electronic devices, to spy on their employees work habits and use of time. They are used in almost every place of business to monitor customer movement and honesty. They provide coverage in parking garages, and gated communities. Police and private security companies constantly monitor shopping malls, parks, public places, and city streets. In many places, your automobile license number and time of day are registered as you arrive and leave private and public places.

The government, using sophisticated electronic devices, can monitor virtually every aspect of your personal life. When you use your cellphone, a computer can record your serial number and location and listen to your conversations to pick up suspicious words and phrases. If any of these words are picked up a file is opened on you and sent to the Department of Homeland Security. If they think you are involved in any suspicious activity they will set up an investigation, wiretap your home, and place you under surveillance. Your cellphone acts as a tracking device and can give your location anywhere within range. Did you know that every movie you rent, or purchase is available for review? If you order adult material that information can be relayed to the taskforce on pornography. Are you going to be out of town for a few days? Did you buy tickets on a plane or train? Did you drive? Did you buy gas or make reservations using a credit card? Did you use an ATM for some cash, and if so, how much? If you answered yes you may have had your movements monitored. Other ways of tracking and monitoring are the use of court and school records, driver's licenses, income tax information, health and banking records. A myriad of other informational sources can be found on the World Wide Web.

The erosion of the Bill of Rights and other unconstitutional acts are manifold. Are you beginning to feel the heavy hand of government intrusion? Did you know that schools are required to give a list of names, addresses, and phone numbers to the Pentagon for the use as a recruiting tool? Failure to do so could result in the withdrawal of federal funding. This provision is neatly tucked away in the No Child Left Behind program. We did not give these rights away! They were taken from us!! The incarceration rate in the United States is the highest in the world. The United States has 24.7% of the worlds prisoners, and 1 in 32 Americans are under criminal justice control. This seems outrageous when the American population is only 5% of the total world population

The privatization of prisons, (for-profit prison industry) has been the leading cause of the increase in incarceration in the United States. There were no private for-profit prisons until the Regan Administration. Inmate populations soared as longer and harsher sentences were handed down. New laws that guaranteed 90% occupancy, known as lock up quotas. States would have to reimburse these newly created for-profit prisons for all the unused beds.

These new "Quota Systems" are mostly filled with the unemployed and the poor, who are safer and easier to convict. White collar crime saw little or no increase, as well as, all other crimes. The prison industrial complex serves two functions; It serves as vehicle of huge profits for their investors, and it serves as a warehouse for surplus labor, and the disenfranchised.

"They hang the man, and flog the woman, who steals the goose from off the common, ----- But turn the greater villain loose, who steals the common from the goose." (An old English rhyme.)

PUBLIC EDUCATION

The purpose of public education is to teach students to function and participate in the free market economy. It can be said that school is an indoctrination center with its order of business set by politicians, and people with their own agendas.

The American dream is presented as an obtainable goal for everyone. The celebration of national holidays and the study of historic events are meant to further cement the impression of a national unity. There are memorials to national heroes, and to wars that promote freedom in the world. The truth and the morality of a great many of these men and events are specious at best. American intervention into the affairs of other nations is well documented.

Schools are designed to resemble a centralized and simulated work place to make the students feel at ease in these surroundings. The school is further divided into rooms in which different subjects are taught. This implants the idea of the specialization of labor. It is the beginning of classifying things, activities, and people into neat little boxes. When one classifies something, it sets boundaries and constraints. This limits thoughts and actions within its definition. This restriction is sometimes called constipated thought. Time is rigidly controlled, and great importance is placed on punctuality. The curriculum's goal is to produce productive workers and to make the students think they are acting in their own best interest. The school's attempt to legitimize the existing educational agenda and control it through a system of compulsory compliance. These ideologies and values are imprinted upon the students under their control to develop the information they need to become useful adults. Emphasis is placed on efficiency and uniformity under the guise of what is socially acceptable. Dissention is not tolerated. The subject of testing students and the assessment of the school's ability to condition the child to perform within specified parameters determines their federal funding or closure. Testing is the procedure that measures the child's ability to solve problems and develop social skills. Testing has become more of an information gathering system about the child's psychological profile than the ability to solve problems. They have all the mechanisms in place for the invasion of privacy. These are the tools set in place for monitoring and tracking political nonconformity, as well as consumer profiling.

Conformity seems to be valued over individualism and imagination. It is much easier to control people by deception, misdirection, omission, and distortion, than by force. It is sad that freethinking and creativity are snuffed out at an early age.

One of the main political objectives in education is to close failing schools. The government has purposed a voucher system to give parents monies to send their children to private schools. This is a bad idea because it uses tax monies for religious instruction in private schools. This is asking Americans to subsidize that which is repugnant to the separation of church and state. Private schools discriminate and reject applications based upon any criteria they choose. These vouchers are of little value if families cannot come up with the rest of the money to cover the cost of tuition. Only the rich and well off middle class students and parents would be the beneficiaries of the lion's share of such a system. Fewer dollars to teach poorer students and further deterioration of the public-school system would be the inevitable result. This would further undermine the education of everyone.

MEDIA

The Federal Communications Commission was created in1934. Its responsibility was to regulate radio broadcasting, telegraph, and telephone services. New technologies broadened their scope to include television, satellite, microwave, and private radio transmissions. The purpose of the FCC was to serve the public interest and enforce standards by licensing or revoking the licenses of those who do not serve the interests of the public. It soon became clear that the FCC favored the interests of big business over those of the public and the community. Over the past years there has been a startling growing trend of media conglomerates controlling what we watch on television, read in the newspaper, and listen to on the radio.

In 1983, 90% of all media in America was owned by 50 companies; the ownership of these companies has now shrunk to only 6 companies. These 6 companies control 90% of everything we watch on TV, listen to on the radio, or read in the newspaper. They are Comcast, Disney, CBS, Time Warner, Viacom, and News-Corp.

We are being force fed a farrago of worthless information, inane and insipid commercials. The airways are filled with the sorted lives of entertainers, sports celebrities, soap operas, and reality shows. Our children are saturated with commercials, violence, and programming designed to shape their minds into servile drones. Little thought is given to educational programing or minority opinions. The BIG 6 also control the content of political and civic issues that further the agendas of the media moguls and the ruling class. The FCC seems to ignore these disturbing trends and gives little thought to the reason why they were created. They no longer serve the interest of the people, and instead concentrate on accommodating big business, and facilitating the consolidation of power into the hands of the elite media. This is a platform for the monopoly of ideas.

Journalists, investigative reporters, and the mainstream press, are the people who inform and shape public opinion. Those who still believe in a free press, and who try to report the truth are often intimidated by the loss of their jobs.

Journalists are expected to acquiesce to the pressure and wishes of the monopolistic media. Truth is censored, marginalized, altered, or just not reported. This leads to an ignorant and misinformed public. I do not use the word ignorant in a disparaging way, it is used to only to imply that they have been misdirected and accept that misdirection as truth. Few of us have the time or resources to personally investigate every news story. We can only rely on what corporate media wants us to hear. This is where the FCC is failing in one of their most important functions, to act in the public interest. The FCC is the regulator of the media and acting in that capacity they have failed the people that they were created to serve. Where else can one go to get a divergent or contrasting opinion? There are a few intrepid individuals and organizations that operate independently of these influences. There are numerous web sites and a few independent broadcasting stations that respond to the truth. Seek them out and keep yourself informed. They are the guardians of your freedom.

FREEDOMS LOST

How did we lose our freedoms? We never lost our freedom, it was stolen from us by the furtive and covert manipulations of the power elite. This oligarchy has shaped our world by defining politically correct thought through propaganda and brain washing. The media plays the most important role because it is the messenger of this assimilated information. People are simply not aware that the opinions they express are the ones they are force fed by media. It is big business and special interest groups that pay media groups to propagandize their viewpoints. Media propaganda is designed to render a response without conscious thought. The specially scripted voices and images ushering forth create the illusion of knowledge and deep insights of well-informed people. They are all guided by acquiescence to the media and those who pull the strings. By design our airways are filled with static and very little substance. They are surfeited with nonsensical and specious advertising and human-interest stories of little interest and no substance. News is distorted and one sided with staged events, photo-ops, imbedded reporters, and dubious figures of authority to explain what you saw. Opposition to these views are deemed to be radical and un-American.

The first democracy is believed to have existed in ancient Athens. In a Democracy, the common people constitute political power, and are represented by free elections. However, slaves, women, and non-property owners were prohibited from engaging in the political process. Does this sound a little familiar? It should. Our founding fathers were of the same mind set. They feared democracy. They believed that the uneducated masses were incapable of governing themselves. Today, to constitute a majority, state legislatures have enacted laws that make minority voting difficult. Voter registration rolls are purged of undesirable voters. Unverifiable electronic voting machines are ubiquitous in the electoral process, along with lost ballot boxes, and long lines in undesirable precincts. Redistricting or gerrymandering is used without restraint.

In the U.S. Constitution article 4 section 4 guarantees every state in the union a republican form of government. When we pledge allegiance to the flag, it is to the republic for which it stands, not to a democracy. It is no wonder that our government is a republic. A republic has a constitution that protects its citizens from the Tyranny of the majority. The constitution has a Bill of Rights that protects its citizens, but it also protects big business which slides under these provisions as "corporations are people too". The Bill of Rights is presently under relentless attack by those who wish to bring down the people. This allows the ruling class to carry on business as usual, with little fear of losing their advantage. Democracy is only majority rule, it does not protect us from the moneyed elite who can buy votes and persuade others to vote against their best interest. A Republican form of government, as well as a Democracy is a double-edged sword, and both protect the moneyed elite, but do little for the people.

In 1954 president Dwight Eisenhower signed into law the phrase "one nation under God" to be added to our pledge of allegiance to the flag.

"In God we trust" first appeared on U.S. coinage in 1864, and in 1957 it appeared on paper money. This seems to be a deliberate assault on the separation of church and state. All this would lead us to believe that some factions in government would lead us into a vision of the U.S. as a Christian nation.

Our vote makes little difference; the choice is either

Tweedledum or Tweedledee. Many third-party candidates do offer a choice, but the two major parties have a stranglehold on the elective process. The average voter has had their vote sullied by the Electoral College. The whole electoral process has been compromised. One solution would be to replace the winner take all Electoral College with a system of Proportional Representation (PR). Voters usually vote for the "lesser of two evils", which leaves them under represented. This under representation leads to voter apathy and low voter turnout. PR does not limit choices to a two-party system but broadens the scope by giving the voters a real choice. PR allows voters to record their second, third, or more choices. If no clear winner emerges with more than 50% of the vote, the candidate with the lowest tally of votes is eliminated, and the second choice on the ballot is then tallied. The process is repeated until a clear winner is created. This strengthens every one's vote and prevents minor candidates from taking votes from the person with the greatest voter support.

Proportional Representation would end redistricting, or gerrymandering. Voting blocks that give political parties an advantage would be made an antiquated practice. Voters falling into economic, ethnic, age, or educational categories, would not be marginalized. The influence of big money would be negated, which would allow more positive and issue related campaigns for voter consideration. PR gives people a real choice. It is a fairer, more effective system, and it is used by most of the world's Democracies. Only a few countries still use the "winner take all" voting system. They are The United States, France, Great Britain, Canada, and India. This form of electoral system is a holdover from colonial times and is designed to keep the oligarchy in place. PR is not perfect, but it comes much closer to a true Democracy than anything else.

Bishop Desmond Tutu says, "the system of Proportional Representation ensures that virtually every constituency in the country will have a hearing in the national and provincial legislature".

A PLEA FOR CHANGE

Change is inevitable. Nothing remains in a state of quiescence. Even forces in apparent equilibrium eventually acquiesce one to the other. Maintaining the status quo will only protract the erosion of our rights. The only solution for society is to undergo a metamorphosis of thought and attitude. Only change can give us back our dignity and freedom. Nations and governments rise and fall in the tides of change. Change can come as a gentle awakening of intellectual awareness or bloody revolution. Other changes include global warming, economic failure, ecological disasters, war, and pandemics. The quality of life is greatly affected by Globalization, population shift, legal and illegal immigration. These forces help change attitudes, and political philosophies.

The American Dream is slowly dying. The frontiers and westward expansion have come to an end. The rugged individualism we held so dear has given way to the pressures of conformity and cooperation. Once there was unlimited opportunity for those who were willing to work hard, and most had a share in the American Dream. The frontiers are gone, and we now find urban blight. Gone are the factories and manufacturing jobs that supported the families of working class Americans. Gone is the opportunity to save enough to send our children to college. Many working Americans are finding that they must work two jobs to support their families. Mothers abandon their traditional roles as homemaker and take full time jobs just to keep their families together. The ruling elite, the lawgivers, and politicians look down from their ivory towers unaware and unmoved by the calamity they have created. All these changes have divided our nation and are rapidly destroying our middle class. There is an ever-widening gap between the rich and poor. We are well on our way to becoming a third world country. Only change tempered with wisdom, logical thought, and the will to act in responsible ways can bring about the demise of hypocrisy and injustice. It is change that will give us a new paradigm to guide and direct our course for the future. We must come to the realization that what we do to the earth, we do to ourselves. What we passively let others do to the earth makes us guilty of the sin of indifference. Earth is the only place in the cosmos that we can call home. We must at all cost keep it a viable place for ourselves and other life forms to evolve the potential within them. This means preserving and developing a functional and sustainable habitat for the diversity of life on our planet. Where is a bill of rights for nature?

The Environmental Protection Agency was created to protect the environment, and its byproduct the quality of life. It was not intended as a vehicle for corporate profit. The EPA has ignored the public outcry, favoring those who pollute our air and water, and use the planet as a toxic waste dump. The corporate elite are quite happy to use our tax dollars for their clean up. It would not be cost effective and would be detrimental to corporate profit if they were required to clean up their own excrement. The people and the planet are in great peril from these pollutants. In many places the quality of the air is unfit to breathe, due to smog. Acid rain, which is mostly caused by the burning of fossil fuels, has contributed to global warming. Toxic sludge is routinely dumped on the land. These bio solids contain a wide variety of toxic chemicals, along with domestic household sewage, and medical waste. The result of this is cancer, disease, genetic mutations, and death, as well as all manner of psychological problems and physical deformities. These toxins not only affect people and animals but their offspring as well. Runoff from the land carries these toxins into our streams, rivers, and lakes, compromising the integrity of our drinking water. Our oceans have also become a dumping ground for every kind of waste and toxic material. This toxic material is destroying the ecosystem and poisoning our food supply. Nuclear proliferation and their deadly byproducts are of worldwide concern. This deadly Hydra will kill, cause cancers, and birth defects in animals and people for years to come. Living organisms cannot tolerate nor endure this transgression on nature and habitat without serious side effects. What greater crime than to allow these infringements on our planet to be done without prohibition? It is much easier to lobby exemptions from the politicians than to do the right thing. This unholy alliance is an anathema, and repugnant to rational thought. No activity that compromises the integrity of our life support system, or that of any other life form, should ever be tolerated.

FUTURE DIRECTIONS

What does the future hold? It is certain there will be change. We can only wonder what incipient ideas and nascent trends are on the horizon? Change is always with us for better or worse.

The increase in the pace of our daily lives leaves us without meaningful choices. If all the extra work was rewarded with greater happiness or gave us a feeling of delight, we might approach it differently.

Technology has heralded in a world we could not have envisioned a century ago. Every field of scientific inquiry has yielded a myriad of new discoveries. Progress and technology has been a two-fold relationship, both a blessing and a curse. The invention of the mechanical cotton picker was said to relieve workers from the drudgery of stoop labor and give them more free time. Well, it did. Cotton farmers bought these machines, and the pickers lost their livelihood. It seems every advance in technology not only has its advantages but also a down side. Few of us would want to give up the miracles of modern medicine, however, we would gladly eschew the expense.

Renewable forms of safe and cost-effective energy to maintain convenience and comfort are a top priority for our future. Most everyone agrees on this premise. However, the implementation of already existing technologies is slow at best. Conservation of petroleum products is only temporary and not a solution. New building techniques and materials offer the promise of energy independence for our homes. Environmentally friendly neighborhoods are already on the horizon.

Things are changing so rapidly it is almost impossible to keep up with all the new technologies. It is difficult to comprehend the significance of all this expanding growth. Our experiences seem to be limited, as we find no frame of reference for many of the new technologies. Nowhere is this more apparent than in the field of computer technologies. In 1948 the Eniac computer came as a miracle of electronic technology. Today's computers are light years ahead in computing power. The Internet revolution has seen a fundamental change in our way of visualizing, processing, and storage of information. Our connection to the World Wide Web is still very young, but its influence on our lives is staggering. One can barely imagine its future implications.

Every day it becomes harder to keep up with the changes that confront us. There is a multitude of distractions that derail and misdirect our focus. We could be poised on the cusp of a new golden age or fall back into the bleak ignorance of the dark ages. We may never experience a perfect Utopian world, but we may someday live lives of freedom and dignity. We no longer wait for evolutionary change. We are now capable, through genetic engineering, of shaping evolution to our own wishes. We must think of our new role as architect in this evolutionary process, and how our actions may affect future generations.

The possibilities of the future stand on the accomplishments of the past. If everything and everyone had to start at the beginning, there would be no progress. It is the achievements of the past that buttress the accomplishments of the future.

These new technologies are the vehicles that will carry us to our future destinations. The basic question remains; how do we relate these new technologies to our wellbeing? The decisions we make must come from rational thought, and must include love, compassion, forgiveness, and self-discipline.

The future is not ours. It belongs to our children. Our children are born into the society we have made for them. They have no choice but to accept the social, religious, and mental attitudes they inherit. We must realize that we live in a world that is limited by the knowledge that others pass on to us. Our children will reflect the same old values, and shopworn traditions, that plague rational thought. Long before we were born others have shaped society and programmed us to obey certain laws and to recognize our obligations within the social structure we inherit. We must somehow escape this stranglehold of conformity. If we do not change, we will carry these old prevailing standards into the future. Or there may be a few courageous and dauntless individuals with the fortitude to formulate a world of their own choosing. These intrepid individuals are our only hope to force the changes necessary to insure everyone has a place of dignity, and that none are left behind. The success of any society can be judged by the quality of life we bequeath to our children. How we structure our society will depend on the choices we make today. What we do here and now will determine the future direction of our species, and perhaps all life on earth.

# # # # # # # # # #

QUOTES IN ORDER OF APPEARENCE

(Jacob Boronski, 1908-1974 mathematician and historian of science) writes in his book, The Ascent of Man, "the hand is the cutting edge if the mind"

(Madalyn Murray O'Hare 1919-1995 The American Atheist), "Atheism may be defined as the mental attitude which unreservedly accepts the supremacy of reason and aims at establishing a lifestyle and ethical outlook verifiable by experience and the scientific method independent of arbitrary assumptions of authority and creeds."

(Isaac Newton) was not the first to use the metaphor, "If I have seen further it is by standing on the shoulders of giants."

Marcus Aurelias, (Roman Emperor from 161 to 180) wrote in his book Meditations "That which has died does not drop out of the universe. If it stays here, it also changes here, and is dissolved in to its proper parts, which are elements of the universe and of yourself, and these too change, and murmur not."

(Friedrich Nietzsche) "The most perfidious way of harming a cause consists of defending it deliberately with faulty arguments."

(Aldous Huxley) Facts do not cease to exist because they are ignored."

(Gandhi) says, "even if you are a minority of one, the truth is the truth."

(Voltaire 1694-1778) observes, "It is dangerous to be right in matters on which the established authorities are wrong."

(Friedrich Nietzsche, the philosopher who is closely associated with Existentialism and Nihilism) writes, "Every belief is necessarily false because there is simply no true world."

(Joseph Goebbels, Hitler's propaganda minister) asserts that, "If you tell a lie big enough and keep repeating it, people will eventually come to believe it".

(Omar Khayyam, Persian poet and astronomer) writes in his book of quatrains, the Rubaiyat, the following observation.

"The Moving Finger writes; and, having writ, ... Moves on: nor all your piety nor Wit. Shall lure it back to cancel half a line. Nor all your tears wash out a word of it." In his play, (As you like it, Shakespeare's character Jacques proclaims), "all the world is a stage and all the men and women merely players."

(Socrates) said, "the unexamined life is not worth living."

(Albert Einstein) writes, "the foundations of morality should not be made dependent on myth nor tied to any authority least doubt about the myth or the legitimacy of the authority imperial the foundation of sound judgment and action."

(Apostle's creed), "I believe in God, the Father almighty, creator of heaven and earth. I believe in Jesus Christ, his only son, our Lord, who was conceived by the Holy Spirit, born of the Virgin Mary, suffered under Pontius Pilate, was crucified, died, and was buried; he descended to the dead. On the third day, he rose again; he ascended into heaven, he is seated at the right hand of the Father, and he will come to judge the living and the dead." (The Catholic Church has added the following.) "I believe in the Holy Spirit, the holy Catholic Church, the communion of saints, the forgiveness if sins, the resurrection of the body, and life everlasting. Amen."

(Pope Gregory 1 540- 604), "Faith has no merit where reason supplies the truth."

(Pope Francis) Leader of the Catholic Church) says, "Money has to serve, not to rule. We have created new idols, the golden calf of old has found a new and heartless image in the cult of money and the dictatorship of an economy which is faceless and lacking any truly human goal. A new invisible and at times virtual, tyranny is established, one which unilaterally imposes its own laws and rules."

(Joseph Goebbels Hitler's propaganda minister from 1939 to1945) states, "If you tell a lie big enough and keep repeating It, people will eventually come to believe it. The lie can be maintained only for such time as the state can shield the people from the political, economic and /or military consequences of the lie. It thus becomes vitally important for the state to use all its powers to repress dissent, for the truth is the mortal enemy of the lie, and thus by extension the truth is the greatest enemy or the state."

"They hang the man, and flog the woman, who steals the goose from off the common .... But turn the greater villain loose, who steals the common from the goose." (An old English rhyme.)

(Bishop Desmond Tutu) says, "the system of Proportional Representation ensures that virtually every constituency in the country will have a hearing in the national and provincial legislature".

(Isaac Asimov 1920-1992) science fiction writer and biochemist) voices this consideration, "Violence is the last refuge of the incompetent."

SUGGESTED READING

JAMES W. SIRE ... The Universe Next-Door.

JACOB BRONOWSKI ... The Ascent of Man ... The Origins of Knowledge and Imagination.

JOSEPH COMPBELL ... The Power of Myth.

DANIEL C. DENNETT ... Darwin's Dangerous Idea ... Breaking the Spell ... Consciousness Explained.

RICHARD DAWKINS ... The Selfish Gene ... The Blind Watchmaker.

SUSAN BLACKMORE ... The Meme Machine.

URSULA GOODENOUGH ... The Sacred Depths of Nature.

ROBERT WRIGHT ... The Evolution of God.

TOM HARPUR ... The Pagan Christ.

MIHALY CSIKSZENTMIHALYI ... The Evolving Self.

CARL SAGAN ... The Demon-Haunted World.

DAVID MILLS ... Atheist Universe.

STEVEN PINKER ... The Stuff of Thought ... Enlightenment Now

VICTOR J. STENGER ... The New Atheism.

SAM HARRIS ... The End of Faith.

ALVIN BOYD KUHN ... Shadow of the Third Century: A Revaluation of Christianity.

HOWARD ZINN ... A People's History of the United States.

ABOUT THE AUTHOR

I am a Secular Humanist, and by saying so, I have placed myself in one of those neat little boxes described in this book. The true nature of who we are does not rest in the nomenclature of any terms or symbols but can only be found outside these restrictive influences.

I am a son to my mother and father, husband to my wife, father to my children, and grandfather to their children. All the people I have known, met, and worked with, have an opinion as to who I am. Each of these people know me from their own frame of reference. How could it be otherwise?

P.A. Ransom

Printed in the United States
By Bookmasters